Dear Job Stressed

Dear Job Stressed

Answers for the Overworked, Overwrought, and Overwhelmed

~~~~~~~~~~~~~~~~

Mary H. Dempcy

Rene Tihista

DAVIES-BLACK PUBLISHING

Palo Alto, California

Published by Davies-Black Publishing, an imprint of
Consulting Psychologists Press, Inc., 3803 East Bayshore
Road, Palo Alto, California 94303; 1-800-624-1765.

Special discounts on bulk quantities of Davies-Black
Publishing books are available to corporations, profes-
sional associations, and other organizations. For details,
contact the Director of Book Sales at Davies-Black
Publishing, 3803 East Bayshore Road, Palo Alto,
California 94303; 415-691-9123; Fax 415-988-0673.

Illustrations by Ed Taber

99 98 97 96   10 9 8 7 6 5 4 3 2 1
Printed in the United States of America

Library of Congress Cataloging-in-Publication Data
Dempcy, Mary, H.
    Dear job stressed ; relief for the overworked, over
wrought, and overwhelmed / Mary H. Dempcy, Rene
Tihista. -- 1st ed.
      p. cm.
    ISBN 0-89106-089-8
    1. Job stress. I. Tihista, Rene II. Title.
    HF5548.85.D46   1996
    158.7—dc20
                   96-21542
                     CIP

FIRST EDITION
First printing 1996

Send me your tired, your weak, your stressed.

Contents

The effects of job stress can be debilitating. People stagger through exhausting work schedules every day and, in many cases, are barely hanging on. Stress affects the quality of both work and home life. We wrote this book because our job stress workshops and the Stress Personalities Model that we have developed over the course of our working careers have made a real difference in people's lives. We seek to bring the skills and stress relief we provided to our clients for years to a broader reading audience, namely you.

Books have been written about the effects of stress, mostly focusing on the health hazards of too much stress. But it's difficult to find a book that deals exclusively with job stress and does so from the employees' perspective—especially one that identifies the most common workplace stressors and provides new strategies and behaviors to apply directly to those stressors.

We developed the Stress Personalities Model in 1976–77 and began giving workshops through college continuing education programs throughout the United States. From day one, we were interested in getting feedback directly from the "horse's mouth." So we left each workshop with briefcases stuffed full of research forms the participants had filled out reporting their stress situations. Poring over these forms, we were able to discover which strategies and behaviors people found most useful. Many participants contributed useful stress relief solutions of their own, which are passed on in this book.

Over the years we collected quite a store of knowledge from a diverse workforce. Our first workbook, *A Guide to Your Stress Personalities,* was published in 1978 and was revised as we gathered new information. It has gone through eleven updates, revisions, and editions. Our first book, *Stress Personalities: A Look Inside Our Selves,* describes the Stress Personalities Model in a broad framework and discusses the process of developing what we call Stress Personalities.

We trained professionals in a wide variety of health care and educational occupations, including physicians, nurses, social workers, dentists, therapists, and schoolteachers. They use the book and workbook to establish a common vocabulary to help themselves and others deal with stress.

Many readers and workshop participants were specifically interested in job stress. They often lamented, "I don't know if work life is really getting more stressful every day or if there is something the matter with me. I need to know how to handle job stress." The focus of our work and research shifted to that arena. Then, in the early 1980s, we added to our client list such industries as high tech, manufacturing, insurance, and finance as well as governmental organizations. Curious to see if the job stresses were different or the same, we did more research. The results were not surprising. People were all feeling the same pressures, regardless of their occupation.

We used the Stress Personalities Model as a template to deal with the most common stress situations people wanted to know how to handle. The outcome is the subject of *Dear Job Stressed: Answers for the Overworked, Overwrought, and Overwhelmed.* The "advice" format used in this book was patterned after our popular e-mail newsletter, *Advice to the Job Stressed.* It seemed the most direct way to analyze a job stress dilemma and provide practical suggestions to the reader without a lot of extraneous theorizing.

One of our most successful techniques is to spice serious subjects with humor. A belly laugh, it has been said, is worth three minutes on a rowing machine. Humor also helps you look at what can seem to be an overwhelming situation in a different light. The concept of Stress Personalities allows people to step back and observe their behavior objectively and even laugh at themselves and the crazy situations we can all get into.

As we wrote the situations you will read in this book, we remembered with fondness the many participants of our programs who had described their experiences with job stress. We also remembered the fun we had role-playing stress and conflict situations. In the style of improvisational theater, we'd ask for a stress situation from the group. It quickly became apparent which Stress Personality was involved, and we'd act out the situation through a humorous skit. The person reporting the problem usually reacted with astonishment and the surprised comment, "That's exactly what's going on. How did you know? You weren't even there." Our reply usually was, "That's true, but the Stress Personalities were."

This self-help book is targeted to those of you who are working longer and longer hours under more pressure. You're the people required to adapt to the now permanent worldwide revolution in the workplace. You are high-tech engineers, programmers, machinists, health care workers, public employees, physicians, sales personnel, telephone support staff, managers, team leaders, shipping clerks, and company owners. We know you because we have been working with people just like you on-site for over twenty years. This book is dedicated to you and all those we've worked with.

CHAPTER 1

To the Job Stressed

Dear Readers,

Y[o]u've survived rightsizing and downsizing without capsizing. Now you're in for reorganization, redeployment, reengineering, and R.I.F., which means reduction in force and could be written RID, as in getting *rid* of you. Those of you not affected by these Orwellian euphemisms are left holding the bag, exhausted, burned out, stressed out, and, in some cases, knocked out with illness. Some of you contract weird immune disorders that your doctors have no names for. Young and outwardly healthy looking, you're told this virus will attack either your bone marrow or your brain. You have to keep your immune system toned, but you're dead tired. Those of you who spend your lives at computer keyboards have your own special hazard: repetitive strain injury, or RSI. Out of a work group of nine tech writers, eight are slowed by RSI and told by their doctors not to type. You're the only one left with two good wrists and ten healthy fingers, and you're afraid you're going to get it, too. Welcome to the modern workplace.

Job stress is exacting a heavy toll on physical and emotional health. Thousands take medication just to make it through the day. Balancing the responsibilities at home and work gets tougher and tougher. You're working longer hours under more pressure than ever because of downsizing. Some corporate cultures promote unrealistic expectations by exhorting you to increase productivity with fewer resources.

Revenue-per-employee requirements constantly escalate, and you're hyped to believe you can do the impossible. When you can't, you feel like a failure, and stress levels increase. Those of you still working watch the attrition of co-workers and wonder if you're next. Fear of losing your job contributes to a sense of economic insecurity. In the midst of all this you're struggling to maintain the "good life"— or in some cases, any life at all.

The majority of you are not plagued by exotic diseases or emotional breakdown. But you are overworked, overwrought, and overwhelmed. Many of you are single parents trying to juggle a career and family. Most of you who are married are both working. Those with no children struggle to find time for each other. Add children to the equation, and people working long hours face additional stress trying to find time for their kids. You feel guilty at work for not being home with them, and guilty at home for not being at work on that critical project your single peers are devoting their all to.

Job Stress—A Fact of Modern Work Life

Stress, like death and taxes, is a fact of life. The only people who don't experience stress are dead people. When you run up a flight of stairs, your body reacts physically. That reaction is a form of stress. When you get angry or feel anxious, your body also reacts, and that, too, is stress. The argument that there is good stress or bad stress is moot. Stress is normal, just as hunger pangs are. If you're trying like mad to lose weight, hunger pangs that drive you to the fridge are a nuisance and could be seen as bad for you. If you're anorexic or tend to stop eating under stress, hunger pangs are a reminder to eat. In that sense, they're "good" for you. The point is they are a normal function of your body. Stress is best looked at the same way. Stress becomes harmful when there's too much of it over a prolonged period of time and you don't know how to manage it.

Along with the good-bad stress argument is the issue of the *source* of stress. Do we create our own stress by our attitudes, perceptions, and behavior, or are there built-in external stressors that we are affected by? One day, before a workshop, we were talking to a trainer who remarked that she didn't believe in the notion of external stressors inherent in a job. "We all create our own stress," she declared. "How can one person handle a so-called stressful job fine, but another falls apart trying to do it?" Her point was that it has to do with the person, not the job.

Interesting question, and one we had been taking a look at. When we first began doing stress programs twenty years ago, we were convinced of the same thing. In fact, the purpose of the *Stress Personalities Model*—described later in this chapter—was to help people see how they caused stress for themselves. We stated then that situations were neutral. For instance, yelling and screaming—is it good or bad? If you're drowning in a lake and someone hears you, it's good. But if you're at the dinner table yelling at your two-year-old for spilling her milk, it's bad. Is the two-year-old causing the stress by spilling her milk, or are you creating your own stress by your reaction? The answer is both.

Over the years, people challenged the idea that situations are inherently neutral, not inherently stressful. People would say, "What about the organization? Isn't it responsible for causing stress by promoting stressful cultures, policies, practices, or procedures? If I were at the beach in Waikiki, I would not be experiencing stress. Sitting at the office with the fourth new boss in six months, who is once more trying to figure out what we're doing, I feel stress. So how is it my fault?" That raises another question: Who is at fault in creating stress? Actually, we have never believed in finding fault.

Few people make themselves miserable on purpose. We're all just doing the best we can. But what we're doing may contribute to or compound stress reactions. For example, I could drive myself nuts sitting on a beach because I can't stop thinking of all the work I have at the office. Or I could be watching with resigned amusement as yet another new manager tries to figure out what she or he is supposed to be doing after yet another reorganization. In this case I'm stressed in Hawaii and relaxed at the office. Therefore I cause my own stress. Sounds good, and we almost believe it. But what shoots a hole in the notion of people causing their own stress is that we've seen countless examples of stressful practices in the workplace, and they are increasing. Employees face pressures and expectations that raise stress and make their jobs tougher. We are asked about how to deal with the same kinds of problems over and over again.

Here's an inherently stressful situation we hear about all the time: The boss marches in dripping with anxiety and says the project deadline has to be moved up because "blah, blah, blah, blah"—all good reasons, of course. You start to protest but stop. You and everyone else in the group know that the deadline you all agreed to a month ago was unrealistic. In fact, some of you were of the opinion that it was "insane." The only reason you didn't say anything at the time was that you didn't want to be seen as a bad sport. Everyone sits in silence. Then someone says enthusiastically, "Well then, we'll just have to push a little harder." But you're already exhausted from pushing hard. A reasonable person might interject here, "I see the necessity but not the possibility. All of us are working weekends and overtime as it is. Would you be willing to let us hire in some help?" "Absolutely not," says the boss. "There are no additional requisitions for more people for this project." Silence again.

At this moment everyone, possibly even the bearer of sad tidings, knows the deadline cannot be met, but nobody says a word. If the thought were the deed and the wish were the fact, you all wish like crazy you could make this new demand come true. But you can't. So it seems you have failure built in to your plans. The deadline is unreachable, but no one can say so.

This very common dilemma is an external stressor. It's true that different people will react in different ways, but did they bring the stress on themselves, or was it built in to the stressful workplace practice? It's a chicken-or-the-egg argument. The point is, people caught in this trap experience intense stress, and it's extremely common. One outcome of this scenario is that people try to make the deadline, bog down, feel like failures, and sometimes get sick. Some quit, morale drops, and the rest stumble along beset by anxiety and stress.

If the deadline is met, this sets off more turmoil. Because of the deadline pressure, everyone knows the product has been shipped with bugs. Banks of response coordinators are necessary to handle the bombardment of furious complaints from customers. Platoons of engineers or product developers feverishly work under intense pressure trying to correct the flaws, and the stress goes up for everyone.

Since most of you have little power to change these stressful business conditions, it's important to get beyond the "Ain't it awful?" view. Yes, people are under enormous pressure to work longer, harder, and for less. That's a fact of life in the workplace these days. We do not propose grand schemes as to how corporate America should fix itself, nor do we want to scold. What we intend to do in this book is to teach working people how to best manage stress under difficult conditions. The good news is, you do have control over yourselves and how you react to job stress.

Job stressors have serious impact on those who don't know how to handle them. Migraines, neck and back aches and injuries, muscle tension, exhaustion, and fatigue are everyday complaints of the job stressed. Emotional pressures, anxiety attacks, depression, anger, loss of interest in the job, burnout, and workaholism are among the many issues tackled in this book. What you need to know is how to handle those everyday workplace stressors that confuse, irritate, frustrate, and debilitate. *Dear Job Stressed* deals with issues and dilemmas most likely to trigger stress on the job and provides tools for handling them through the template of the Stress Personalities Model. This stress behavior model is designed to help you deal with the stress you create yourself as well as the external stressors inherent in today's workplace.

The Stress Behavior Feedback Loop

A quirk many people exhibit when trying to solve a problem is to act in a way that either doesn't work or makes the problem worse. Then they fruitlessly continue the behavior even though it escalates the stress. For instance, you try to be nice to someone who's being nasty to you, and the nicer you are the nastier they become. So your solution is to be even nicer, which makes the other person even nastier. In stressful circumstances the nervous strain and pressure you feel fog your thinking. You try to handle the pressures by reacting with familiar, though not necessarily helpful, coping behaviors. Stress behavior feeds on itself. The more stress you feel, the more you use the stress-producing behavior.

Why do people doggedly insist on responding to a stressful event in a way that doesn't work and even increases the stress? The answer is that the behaviors have become automatic, habitual patterns you are not consciously aware of. Perhaps they worked at one time and in some circumstances still do. But when they increase stress, and you keep using them, you are caught in a *stress feedback loop*.

These behaviors are generated by Stress Personalities—normal attitudes, beliefs, and response patterns that are identified and discussed in this book. There are seven of them including the Pleaser Stress Personality. The following example describes how a Stress Personality contributes to the feedback loop process.

Let's say you're a customer service representative and receive calls from frustrated, sometimes angry customers all day long. You try to handle them through your Pleaser Stress Personality. You promise a quick response to their pleas but can't deliver because the engineers who are supposed to fix the product can't, or they are too busy to accommodate you. The customer calls back angrier, and you make more promises you can't keep in order to pacify the angry caller. You still can't deliver, and the customer is now furious as you try to explain, apologize, and express your mortification at disappointing the caller. Your stress increases, especially when the angry customer calls your manager to complain about you. Now everyone is after you like hounds after a rabbit.

Your Pleaser has an overriding need to pacify and make sure nobody is angry or disappointed. This part of you is directly responsible for making those promises you can't deliver because of the misconception that if you tell people what they want to hear, they'll be happy and leave you alone. This is how a Stress Personality causes stress.

The Stress Personalities Model

All Stress Personalities have their own psychology and react from their own belief systems and agendas, independent of your conscious awareness. We call them personalities because each is a behavior pattern with recognizable traits that can be identified and even measured. By giving the patterns names we bring them to conscious awareness. When you are able to recognize the Stress Personality and its habitual quality, you have a choice as to how to moderate it.

Because Stress Personalities are normal patterns people use to try to cope with stress, you will recognize yourself in many if not all of them. They are not good or bad. This is not a religious model. They are "bad" only when causing excessive stress, as described in the letters of the "Advice columns" later in this book. If the Stress Personalities were not causing difficulties, there would be no reason to change the behavior.

As you read the following capsule descriptions you will see yourself and others you know in the patterns. It's a good way to begin understanding the Stress Personalities Model.

These descriptions will be expanded on in each chapter so that you will get to know your Stress Personalities intimately. That way you can decide if and when you want them as "inner bedfellows." As you read these descriptions, notice if they remind you of anyone, or if you behave this way under stress.

PLEASER

Pleaser is the facet of your personality that wants to be pleasant, accommodating, cooperative, helpful, and nice to be around. We all like a pleasant work environment free of contention and full of camaraderie. For Pleaser, in a non-stressful mode, being accommodating to others is a pleasure. But when there are too many demands, the stress rises and pleasure turns to resentment.

The behavior causes stress when you can't take care of both others and yourself. According to Pleaser, someone has to be sacrificed, and you're always the lamb. Resentment follows because your Pleaser is giving you away while another part of you feels cheated and laments, "It isn't fair. Why do we always come last?"

STRIVER

Striver is the Stress Personality that fuels the ambition that drives achievement needs. Everyone wants to succeed. A child's first stumbling steps are Striver driven. So is the urge to compete and win. But, if not tempered, this powerful part of yourself takes over. Striver insists you need to excel at everything to stay ahead of others on the fast track. Never satisfied with current effort, Striver continually raises the bar. You impose increasingly high standards on yourself. The result is, nothing is good enough, average equals failure, and being the elusive Number One becomes the glittering goal on the horizon. Perfection is demanded, even under the most imperfect conditions. "After all," says Striver, "someone as outstanding, brilliant, innovative, and eloquent as you should never settle for less." Because of the need to climb the achievement ladder at all costs, Striver pushes you relentlessly to prove yourself.

CRITICAL JUDGE

Critical Judge is your internal assessor. Its job is to determine the significance and value of what you do. In balance, the measurement is objective and not stress provoking. When skewed, however, the readings are exclusively negative. As with a thermometer that reads only sub-zero temperatures, positive assessments are not registered. "Why do you have to look at what you're doing right? That's ridiculous," reasons Critical Judge. This Stress Personality believes that self-improvement will come only from concentrating on your mistakes.

Such a view produces an overemphasis on the negative under the misconception that self-flagellation will motivate you to do better. This overzealous fault finder produces the opposite effect. You lose motivation and are prone to give up and say, "What's the use; I can never do anything right."

INTERNAL TIME-KEEPER

Internal Timekeeper is a good source of energy. It revs you up and gets you going. As work pressures increase, however, you throw more balls in the air than you can juggle. This Stress Personality urges you to get busy and stay busy, because a busy person is sure to be successful. Inevitably you end up with too much to do and too little time. Anxiety and stress scatter your attention, and jobs get misplaced and have to be done over. This duplication of effort wastes time and decreases efficiency and productivity. Doing something every moment at work and at home is a virtue to this Stress Personality. When you try to rest or relax, you imagine the specter of yourself as a lazy bum, and anxiety drives you to your feet. You plunge yourself into another round of hectic activity prodded by this inner speed demon.

SABER-TOOTH

Sabertooth represents all the forms of anger that are ordinarily generated during a stress-filled day. Getting angry when pushed by too much work or constant interruptions is not unusual. Sabertooth characteristics can take such benign forms as friendly, humorous insults or sarcastic greetings between co-workers.

However, when stress gets out of hand, Sabertooth begins to push the envelope. Anger builds and spills out whether you want it to or not. You walk around with a chip on your shoulder. Anger directed at the wrong person, free-floating hostility, yelling fits of rage, and hostile remarks at those Sabertooth believes are "out to get you" can be hazardous to your career. These abrasive, belligerent features are not attractive to or esteemed by others. Because Sabertooth is not easy to acknowledge in yourself, it's common to develop a blind spot and fail to recognize the potential destructiveness of the behavior.

WORRIER

Worrier is the self-appointed guardian of your security. Ambiguous circumstances like fuzzy job descriptions, unclear instructions, and vague or contradictory goals set off "security anxiety," a fear of the unknown and uncertain. Because Worrier imagines the worst possible outcomes, worry becomes the process to prevent unforeseen disasters. Everybody worries, but when worry displaces problem solving with obsessing, you move up the stress continuum. A definition of *obsessing* includes repeatedly seeking reassurance but not taking it in, and fussing over detail to the point of immobilization.

Another stress behavior is the need to compile so many facts before making a decision that you stay in a constant state of ambivalence. Worrier cautions, "It's better to make no decisions than the wrong one." Worrier's goal is to be sure you worry enough to be totally prepared for any contingency. If you are, you can't be surprised with bad results. From this stressful perception, the more you worry, the safer you'll be.

INNER CON ARTIST

Inner Con Artist refers to conning yourself by making up rationalizations to justify self-defeating behavior. "If I avoid tough personal problems they'll eventually disappear" is one, and "I don't get paid enough to kill myself on this job" is another. This part of yourself is always watchful that you don't work too hard. "All work and no play, after all, make Jack a dull boy," says Inner Con Artist. This Stress Personality sees itself as the antidote to workaholism and often emerges as a symptom of burnout. When you resemble a pile of cinders, Inner Con Artist takes over, trying to counteract the stress of pushing too hard. But the shortcoming of using this fix is that Inner Con Artist has no limits or balance. You will be led down the path of excessive self-indulgence, lose self-control, and do just enough work to get by. While it's true all work and no play make Jack a dull boy, unfortunately all play and no work make Jack unemployed.

The object of labeling stress behavior is not to point fingers or put you in a box. It's to give you a way to categorize your automatic stress responses in order for you to control them more effectively. A question we are asked frequently is, "I recognize myself in each of these Stress Personalities. Is that possible?" The answer is yes. These are normal behaviors and are *parts* of yourself, not *who* you are. We encourage you to look at them as separate entities.

Parts of the Self: "Now You See Me, Now You Don't"

In order to apply this model of stress reduction in your everyday life, it is crucial to understand the concept of "parts of the self." What do we mean by this? It's common to hear people say, "I said to myself," or "I got so mad at myself," or "I should have listened to myself." The question is, who is the "I" and who is the "self" they were talking to? Just as you talk to yourself all the time, you also talk to your Stress Personalities. The model gives these "parts" a name and identity that make it easier to relate to them. We have all had the experience of another part of us taking over without our being aware of it. An example is driving from home to work and realizing you weren't even conscious of how you got there. Somebody was at the wheel; you arrived safely. That driver was your automatic pilot. Our Stress Personalities are also automatic pilots. You have to bring them to consciousness to control them so you don't crash.

Unlike some other personality models that name patterns, the Stress Personalities Model does not suggest that a part of yourself is who you are. You are not a Striver, Pleaser, Sabertooth, and so on. At work, you may go into Striver mode, big time. At home, with your kids, you might be a pussycat Pleaser and let them manipulate you. A phone call from a parent immediately brings out Critical Judge, and you begin defending yourself. Behind the wheel of your car you could be a raging Sabertooth. But when you get to work, you're known as the old "soft touch" Pleaser whom anyone can rely on to help them get their tasks done, even though it puts you behind schedule.

Another important point to recognize is that it's not uncommon for Stress Personalities to work together or set each other off. When you please, please, please and never say no to people who dump work on you, you shift into Internal Timekeeper in order to get all the work done. Now your stress and overwork are caused by *two* Stress Personalities. To reduce the stress, focus on Pleaser and Internal Timekeeper will automatically diminish.

Sometimes you can be mistaken as to which Stress Personality is causing the biggest headache. Never fear; the right one will emerge. A very successful salesman in one of our workshops, who called himself "the best salesman in the world," was upset with his Inner Con Artist. Every night he came home with a briefcase full of work to be done. It was usually around 8 P.M. and he was tired and hungry. He'd sit down in front of the TV with a snack to watch the news before he got to the work he'd brought home. He immediately fell asleep and would wake up in the middle of the night with a fuzzy, discombobulated feeling, which prevented him from tackling his briefcase full of work. Then he'd go to bed irritated with himself.

During the workshop he discovered to his amazement that his struggle was actually more with his Striver. Inner Con Artist was the secondary Stress Personality. He was working a killer schedule, with no letup and no time for friends or fun, and was exhausted. He wouldn't slow down. So his Inner Con Artist took over and slowed him down.

But when faced with the inevitable truth that to control his Inner Con Artist, he had to modify his Striver, he backed away out of fear that he would lose his coveted title, "best salesman in the world." Unless he learns to deal with his Striver, his Inner Con Artist will lay him low whether he likes it or not.

A Bridge to Your Inner Selves

The concept of separate entities that you talk to within yourself is extremely effective in controlling behavior you wish to manage better. It is also normal to talk to yourself—and answer. It's not crazy, as is frequently supposed. The most intelligent people problem-solve this way. You'll notice in the upcoming Advice sections that we often say, "Tell your Stress Personality to back off." Or we might advise, "Don't take your Pleaser along when you want to ask for a raise." This objective stance separates you from the Stress Personality and gives you a measure of immediate control. It also gives your unconscious the message that if this is only a part of yourself, there is another part that can take charge of the situation and the Stress Personality.

As you begin to talk to them, to decide whether to use their services or not or to override their decisions, you are forming a relationship with them. It's this bridge between the conscious and unconscious that provides you with influence over them. Stress Personalities communicate with us during stressful times. You can learn which one is talking by paying attention to your thoughts and actions.

How Stress Personalities Cause Stress

Stress Personalities are normal because stress is normal. But when stress increases daily, unrelentingly, and over an extended period of time, performance and even health can suffer. A helpful way to look at how stress moves from the normal range to the hazardous range is to see stress on a continuum from low to high.

Low ——————————————————————————————————— High

STRESS CONTINUUM

The following example shows how a Stress Personality oscillates a salesman from the low to the high end of the stress continuum and threatens a big sale.

Peter is a successful salesman. Typically, salespeople demonstrate a lot of Sabertooth characteristics. They have to be aggressive and doggedly persistent, make demands, and ask for the business. They can sometimes be seen by others as pushy. Peter has a big contract pending with a customer who is choosing between his company and another. He has an inside contact who got him in the door. His Sabertooth Stress Personality helped him stay in the running with proactive determination to win the contract. The word from his inside contact strongly suggests he'll get the sale.

However, he starts to get uneasy. The decision is taking longer than he expected. When he calls they seem to put him off. Now he's suspicious and begins calling more frequently. He gets perilously close to badgering his inside connection, who starts to show annoyance with him. This makes him more anxious. His sales lead tells him to back off for a few days. But Peter's Sabertooth won't let him and warns that he is getting aced out or brushed off. So he increases the number of calls until his inside contact tells him that if he keeps this up, he will lose the sale.

This is a good example of how a Stress Personality is beneficial when the behavior remains at the low end of the continuum. But as the stress increases, and Peter uses more and more Sabertooth, he moves to the high end. Sabertooth stops being beneficial and becomes a detriment. Aggressive persistence becomes intrusive badgering. Before Peter could change, he had to recognize that his Sabertooth was driving his actions.

Stress Personalities Render the Unpredictable Predictable

You will respond to different stressors with different Stress Personalities. However, the responses are not random. It's predictable that certain conditions will bring out a particular Stress Personality. The key is to figure out which ones you tend to use in response to particular situations. This adds predictability and keeps you from being caught off guard and ambushed by the unforeseen. A common complaint is, "I can handle stress unless I'm hit with something unexpected." People want to know how to prepare themselves before stress waylays them.

For example, people who dread speaking in front of groups are uncomfortable because of their Critical Judge. The inner voice of this Stress Personality can be counted on to critique your performance in a negative way, which raises stress and makes matters worse. If you know this, you can counter Critical Judge's influence by warding off the voice of negative criticism while you're speaking. Or say you're faced with an unreasonable deadline and already feeling time-pressured anxiety. Your Internal Timekeeper urges you to hurry up, insisting that you have so much to do that you're never going to make it otherwise. Increased agitation causes you to forget what you are doing, lose track of where you are, make mistakes, and reduce your efficiency. When you're aware that

Internal Timekeeper accelerates during these periods of pressure, you can slow yourself down and concentrate.

If Stress Personalities cause stress, why, you might ask, do we rely on them? The answer can be found in our attitudes, beliefs, and perceptions of the world.

What You See Is What You Get: Stressful Perceptions

Stress Personalities produce stress behavior because of belief systems. A stressful perception is a habitual belief of a Stress Personality and is tied to basic survival. The attitudes and the reactions produced from them seem to serve us, or so we think. Therefore a seemingly bizarre behavior, such as worrying over things you can do nothing about, emanates from the desire to insure yourself a safe future. The wish for security is perfectly normal, but no amount of worrying can insure it. Even such seemingly negative self-talk from Critical Judge as "You never do anything right" or "You are a miserable failure" is an effort to motivate you to do better.

However, constant negative self-criticism is stressful and doesn't motivate but saps enthusiasm. People act from stressful perceptions every day of their lives because they believe the behavior they're manifesting is absolutely necessary to get what they want.

A manager says, "In order to get my point across I have to yell." This is a Sabertooth stressful perception. The assumption that she has to yell to make others listen automatically raises her stress. She's accepted the validity of her Stress Personality's certainty that hollering your way through the workday is the only way to get others to hear you.

A program director says, "If you are not constantly striving and achieving, you won't be successful." This attitude drives workaholism, prevents him from having a balanced life, and incessantly pressures him to do better. The conviction that there is no middle ground between constant achievement and failure makes for a very narrow bandwidth of behaviors. From this perspective he can easily mistake exhaustion and burnout for laziness, and push himself harder when he really needs to slow down.

As you read the Advice sections in this book, you will encounter many stressful perceptions of the Stress Personality under discussion. They explain and amplify why the person is using the particular stress behaviors. As you familiarize yourself with the various perceptions, you will be able to quickly identify your own that crop up during similar occurrences.

When stressful perceptions are identified, the next step is to consider another way to look at the situation. It's exciting to discover a brand-new take on a seemingly bewildering predicament or state of mind.

New Perceptions: "Ah Hah!"

New perceptions are a new way to regard a stressor from another perspective, free of the Stress Personality's influence. Sometimes they come out of the blue, as an "Ah Hah" experience. Perhaps it's a sudden realization that an impossible person or intractable condition is never going to change just because you want it to happen. So you have to accept it and take care of yourself the best way possible. New perceptions ease stress. They give you a unique view of things. For example, in a conflict, replacing a stressful perception with a new perception can shine a new, non-contentious light on things. Someone you saw from Critical Judge as rude, abrasive, and insulting is really reacting from Internal Timekeeper and is abrupt because she or he is busy and harried. Viewed in this light, it's understandable. Resolution is often the result when you substitute new perceptions for the stressful perceptions that are provoking the conflict. In fact, giving the behavior patterns the name Stress Personalities is itself a new perception.

Stress Situation: Who's in the Driver's Seat?

Here is a simple illustration showing how a new perception takes the stress out of a conflict. A couple who commute together always clash over their driving habits. They are prone to making sarcastic remarks about each other's driving skill.

"Darn, honey, you missed sideswiping that car. You're losing your touch," says the passenger.

"Who's holding the wheel? I don't need your advice on how to drive this car," the driver retorts.

This bickering is known as backseat driving. In our programs over the years we've trained many people from other cultures who may not recognize the term but definitely recognize the conflict. "We do the same thing in our country," they always say with a smile, "but it has a different name." Obviously, backseat driving is a global stressor. It's stressful enough commuting to work in heavy traffic; you don't need a fight to make matters worse. This common conflict is unnecessary, and it can be resolved with a simple new perception that will show you how to compromise and control road stress and other "auto-erratic" behaviors.

In this case, Critical Judge is in the passenger's seat and Sabertooth behind the wheel. The stressful perception of the passenger is that "nagging will correct driving inadequacies." The driver's is, "I'm captain of the ship, so you have to keep your mouth shut." Neither of these attitudes works to insure a safe and pleasant journey.

Another Way to Look: Co-Driving Smoothes the Bumps

A new perception that would help remedy this stress-inducing conflict is, "No matter who's driving, an accident could injure or kill both of us. So we each have a responsibility for our safety." This allows them to coin a new definition of backseat driving and call it "co-driving." The name unloads the critical label of backseat driver. A co-driver, just like a co-pilot on an airplane, is helpful and necessary. Another new perception is, when someone gives you road information it's not nagging, it's helpful. These perceptions lead to new behavior that will reduce road stress.

One example of a new behavior resulting from this new perception would be for the driver to thank the co-driver when road hazards are pointed out. If you're the passenger and see potential danger, you don't scream, stomp your foot on an imaginary brake, or grab the steering wheel. Instead, you act in a new way you've both agreed on. "Careful, this guy is changing lanes and talking on a car phone," you say calmly. Or you use hand signals to let the driver know about erratic drivers.

New perceptions are an important stress reducer. The Advice sections will pinpoint those for each Stress Personality involved. These new outlooks by their nature suggest new behaviors. You will see in Chapter Five how a financial analyst, pushed by his Internal Timekeeper to take on more work than he is capable of within a given time frame, can apply the new perception that you can't stretch time so you have to shrink work. His new behavior? He begins to prioritize his "To Do" list.

In Chapter Two, a supervisor who reacts with Pleaser to a difficult, unhappy subordinate who has mood swings discovers a new perception. Instead of feeling responsible for making the subordinate feel better, as her Pleaser is urging, the supervisor decides, "It's not my job to be her personal friend but to be her manager." This prompts her to lay out clear performance expectations for her subordinate.

Advice to the Job Stressed

While each Advice column deals with a specific topic, the Dear Readers sections generalize to encompass issues you'll readily recognize in your own life. You'll learn to get a grip on these high-stress dilemmas and how to apply the Stress Personalities Model to additional stress situations.

All the concepts discussed thus far are used in the advice sections to analyze the letters from advice seekers and provide stress tips. The objective of the Advice sections is to help you recognize typical stressful situations, identify the Stress Personality driving the problem, and challenge the stressful perceptions fueling the reactions. Once you've done this, new perceptions will enable you to apply the suggested stress tips to your own needs.

Stress Tips: New Behaviors

New behaviors are different actions or strategies based on a new perception used to handle a stressful predicament or resolve a conflict. All the stress tips suggested in the columns are specific to a particular Stress Personality. The tip "Stand up for yourself" is essential for reducing Pleaser stress, but unnecessary for Striver or Sabertooth. "Focus on the positive" is important for Critical Judge, but not necessarily for Pleaser, who wears rose-colored glasses. New behaviors in general work best when applied to a particular Stress Personality.

Strategies that have proven effective in handling specific stress situations are provided throughout the book. A particular tip is linked to the Stress Personality under discussion. The stress tips included come from our work and research. They have been tried and proven successful. In our workshops and seminars we've gathered more information and stress- reducing alternatives that people find effective. We pass them along to you. Responses to our newsletter *Advice to the Job Stressed,* sent out over the Internet, bring replies and suggestions as well from people who've never been through our programs. They find the stress tips we suggest work. And so will you.

How to Read This Book

Each chapter begins with a composite scenario of a stressed-out employee at work in typical circumstances that trigger the Stress Personality. A discussion of how the Stress Personality causes stress and a Stress Test of ten questions follow. These ten questions represent typical beliefs and behaviors of the Stress Personality that increase stress. When you answer them, it will help you understand how much this Stress Personality influences you and how frequently you react to that influence. Next comes an introduction that describes the topics of the Advice columns. The topics introduce the main concern discussed in the letters.

The answers to the inquiries and the Stress Tips are specific to the problem presented, but are generic to the topic under discussion. The Dear Readers summaries expand on the topic. The Dear Readers Postscripts deal with the Stress Personality in general and how it relates to your work, home life, health, and relationship to your job.

If the primary source of your job stress comes from your fear of saying no to those taking advantage of you because you're afraid to hurt someone's feelings, start with Chapter Two. You'll learn how your Pleaser helps everyone to have a nice day except you.

Those of you who are workaholics and are unable to pass up any opportunity because it could be the "big one" better start with Chapter Three and meet your running partner, Striver.

If you never seem to be quite good enough either at home or work, no matter how hard you try, Chapter Four is a good place to start challenging your Critical Judge.

Those of you too overwhelmed to finish anything and who find yourselves on a treadmill of escalating activity and endless tasks, meet your Internal Timekeeper in Chapter Five.

Chapter Six discusses aggression, anger, impatience, and a relationship conflict. Start here if you're angry a lot and if commuting to work brings out the Sabertooth in you.

If chronic ambivalence, fear of job insecurity, indecision, and worry about the future plague you, start with Chapter Seven and meet Worrier. If you've already made Worrier's acquaintance in the middle of the night, this chapter will be a good sedative.

Chapter Eight is the chapter to begin with if you've been wanting to read a book on job stress for a long time but keep putting it off. You'll meet the master procrastinator, Inner Con Artist, whose motto is, "Anything worth doing is worth putting off."

If you're overworked, overwrought, and overwhelmed, you'll need to gain a fresh perspective on job stress. It's time to gain mastery of your life. Read on and meet the Stress Personalities in action.

CHAPTER 2

Pleaser

No Is Not a Four-Letter Word

How to Recognize *Pleaser*

It's one of those days. Barry has been deluged with demands since he walked in to work at 7 A.M. He came in an hour earlier today, hoping to get caught up from yesterday. Determined to get some relief from the constant desperate pleas for help from co-workers, he put up a "Do Not Disturb" sign outside his cubicle. Everyone ignored it. He even drew menacing jagged letters so it would look fierce and formidable. Still, everyone ignored it.

Barry doesn't know how to get people to respect his right to have some time to himself. He has tried to be firm, pleasant, and courteous, but his co-workers just don't get the message. His main source of trouble is that he has to get his own work completed while being available to handle work others bring him. Barry fears that he will be marked down on his evaluation or fired if he doesn't get everything done. He has taken to hiding in a breakout room, leaving the lights off so no one will know he is in there. The disadvantage of this strategy is that he is not at his workstation, where his work is. He can't see that well in the dim light of the breakout room either, and someone always finds him anyway.

Barry is afraid people won't like him if he doesn't take care of their needs. This is stressful for him because he doesn't have time to do everything. There are too many needs and only one Barry. He can't understand why people seem to single him out to demand things when others can say no and get away with it. The reason? Barry has a strong and stress-producing Pleaser.

THE *PLEASER* STRESS TEST

Read the questions below and place a check (✔) in the appropriate column to the right to indicate your response. Find out how your Pleaser beliefs and behaviors increase your stress. Pay attention to the questions you checked "Usually" and "Frequently." These have to be reduced to "Occasionally" or "Seldom" in order to control Pleaser.	NEVER	SELDOM	OCCASIONALLY	FREQUENTLY	USUALLY
Do I: 1. Have trouble saying no to excessive demands? 2. Believe that if I say no I won't be liked? 3. Avoid confrontations with stronger personalities? 4. Give in when I don't want to? 5. Feel responsible for keeping up office morale? 6. Try to be all things to all people? 7. Pick up the slack from others who aren't doing their share? 8. Allow myself to be manipulated when under pressure? 9. Avoid conflict rather than deal with it? 10. Believe it doesn't matter if I'm happy as long as everyone else is?					

How *Pleaser* Causes Stress

An obsession with fairness plagues Pleaser. The Pleaser golden rule is, "If I give to others they will reciprocate without my having to ask. People should be nice, decent, and caring." But when they aren't, the giving gets lopsided and the getting doesn't happen. You feel used, and stress increases as you feel deprivation, anger, and disappointment.

When you are continually perceived by others as the one who gives, that becomes your identity. Getting is not part of that identity. But your Pleaser secretly holds out the hope that if you just give enough you will be loved. Being loved means survival, self-esteem, security, and success. To say no threatens these basic survival needs, and it feels like you're going against your own best interests.

Advice to the Job Stressed

This chapter focuses on four different high-stress situations that are frequently reported to us as workplace stressors for Pleaser. The first example, "Space Man Alienated," describes how a space allocation coordinator is squeezed by the demands of colleagues seeking office space when there's not enough room to accommodate them. The advice suggests how to change the focus from trying to make everyone happy to just doing your job.

In "Airhead Seeks Breathing Room," an administrator is afraid to speak up when her work load gets so huge that she loses productivity. Rather than hurt anyone's feelings, she lets colleagues dictate her work priorities. The stress tips show how to ask for help when it's needed.

Reluctance to address a nagging conflict that needs to be resolved is the subject of "The Insubordinate Subordinate." Because Pleaser dreads conflict, the hope is it will resolve itself, but proactive engagement is necessary to end a job war.

In "Support Engineer Tilts at Windmills," the subject is how to overcome your Pleaser's reluctance to say no. You'll find out that pushing back is not necessarily an impossible dream.

Everyone has to deal with these high-stress predicaments. Read the following topic introductions and the "Dear Mary and Rene" letters. The replies to these letters show you how to reduce the stress of typical Pleaser dilemmas.

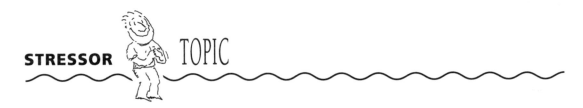

STRESSOR TOPIC

HOW TO STOP TRYING TO MAKE EVERYBODY HAPPY

It's axiomatic that you can't please everyone, yet a surprising number of people in the workplace try anyway. Some try because they feel intimidated by an overpowering boss or co-worker. Others feel guilty when they have to disappoint someone. And still others actually think that if they try hard enough, they can make everyone happy, all the time. No matter what the motive, it's impossible to please everyone. Someone is bound to be upset, and the rancor that follows is stressful for Pleaser. In the following letter, a space allocation coordinator gets himself into a no-win bind trying to please everybody. Rather than disappoint others, his Pleaser allows them to take advantage of him.

Space Man Alienated

> *Dear Mary and Rene,*
> *I handle the space allocation for two groups besides my own. There are many people involved, and I'm responsible for both following the guidelines and trying to keep everybody happy. There is always someone who is*

unhappy and wants me to bend the rules. I juggle office space for one person only to be harangued by someone else who demands their space needs be met first. I get defensive and try to explain how difficult it is to arrange space. I try to stand firm but, under the relentless pressure, give in and bend the rules for the loudest mouth. Then someone else finds out I bent the rules and squawks, which makes me feel guilty and more defensive.

After a day trying to arrange everyone else's space, I feel alienated and just want to be left alone. At home I withdraw from my family. All I want is my own space. When I'm under these stressful conditions my wife says I'm hard to live with. I feel guilty, irritable, crabby, snappy, and moody. I have trouble falling asleep because I'm anxious. I worry because I could get into trouble for not following the guidelines. How do I follow the rules and keep everyone happy?

When You Say Yes You Feel Used

Dear Space Man,

There is no job description that includes a mandate to keep everyone happy all the time, sacrificing yourself in the bargain. That is, unless it's written by your Pleaser. Concern for the happiness and well-being of others is noble. But be aware that the underlying reason to keep everybody happy is so that they won't be upset or angry with you. Pleaser hates conflict even when it's benign. Despite Pleaser's strenuous efforts to make sure everyone has a nice day, there will always be somebody under a dark cloud.

Below are Pleaser traits that sabotage you in your space conflict. Ask yourself if you are:

- Unwilling to stand your ground when challenged
- Tormented with guilt when you have to say no
- Allowing others to take advantage of you

To change stressful behavior, identify the stressful perceptions of Pleaser and substitute new perceptions that allow new behaviors. For example, a Pleaser stressful perception is, "I cannot be happy unless everyone around me is happy." This is a stress-producing belief because it puts you into an impossible bind. You can please some of the people some of the time, to paraphrase Abe Lincoln, but you cannot please all of the people all of the time.

Your wife's feedback is proof of this. She's complaining. Obviously you're not pleasing her. She's getting the fallout of you being Mr. Nice Guy all day. In order to avoid conflict, you are taking a lot of flack from people. When you do this, tension builds. The amount of anger you express at home is a gauge as to how ineffective you feel at handling this stress situation at work.

To transport yourself out of this "space war," put into practice the following stress tips.

STRESS TIPS SPACE MAN COMES TO EARTH

Use the rules and regulations to help you set limits.

When you can't give someone what they want and have to say no, an effective variation on saying no outright is to use the guidelines to say no for you. When people ask you to ignore the rules, inform them that you've been instructed to follow them. For example, you can say: "I understand how you could be upset because I can't bump someone else and give you their space, but I'm required to follow the rules." Make it clear, however, that they can take it to a higher space authority (perhaps the Federation starship captain).

Acknowledge concern but avoid defensive responses.

Defensive responses make you more susceptible to manipulation. Your defensive reaction sets off guilt and remorse. This makes you vulnerable to doing what you said you wouldn't do: bend the rules and let those badgering you have their way. When you give in you are apologizing for your defensiveness. Instead, acknowledge concern for others' needs but hold your ground. For example, you could say, "I understand your dilemma and I'm sorry." Then leave it at that.

Address demands without taking them personally.

It is a Pleaser trait to take everything personally. The objective fact is that everyone wants their space and space is always limited. It's normal for people to get mean and cranky when their territorial imperative is threatened. Detach yourself from the feelings of your co-workers and focus on the outcome. It's your job to find space for people, not to make them happy.

Stress Tips Summary

When Space Man follows these tips he'll introduce balancing steps to counter Pleaser's influence. He'll practice being more direct, use the structure of the guidelines already set up for him, and stop apologizing for doing his job. When he follows these tips at work, he won't be Darth Vader at home. Then he can consider crabby, snappy, and moody to be a wonderful name for an Addams family breakfast cereal instead of a way to relate to his family. When he stands on terra firma, the space war will vanish at warp speed.

TOPIC SUMMARY

The Stress of Trying to Make Everybody Happy

Dear Readers,

Often people are told that to reduce stress, "Just don't take things so personally." Easier said than done. Especially for Pleaser. This Stress Personality has a soft spot. It's a caring energy, but it gets tangled up when the work focus is on other people's feelings. Of course you want to generate good will, but Pleaser is overloaded in that direction. To regain balance, accept the fact that you are at work and your primary goal is to focus on work outcomes, not on people's feelings.

It's common for some support personnel to be responsible for providing service for as many as fifty or more colleagues, each under pressures of their own. When you're beleaguered by demands from frantic co-workers, it's difficult to say, "Whoa." Tempers fray under these conditions and stress is high. The only hope you have is to put your responses in some kind of order. Setting limits as to how much you can take, and being clear about it, is one way to create order. Another is to set priorities when all about you are demanding theirs. One way to do this is to stop trying to do everything yourself and ask for help.

STRESSOR TOPIC

SETTING PRIORITIES WHEN EVERYONE WANTS TO BE FIRST

Pleaser will hamper you from setting work priorities when they clash with the needs of others. Colleagues get indignant and demand their schedules be met first. So you give in and convey the message that you will meet everyone's demands, because you're reluctant to hurt anyone's feelings.

Without establishing priorities that are clear to you and co-workers, you give the message that you will be able to meet everyone's demands. When you can't, you're vulnerable to the stress of reacting to those who are most vociferous, the "squeaky wheels." After all, frets Pleaser, to set a priority means some things are more important than others. One person's need will be superseded by someone else's. The second person will be disappointed, and this makes your Pleaser very uncomfortable. So once more you rush to the rescue. In the next letter, "Airhead" takes on everything dumped on her so that no one has to be displeased.

Airhead Seeks Breathing Room

Dear Mary and Rene,

I have a constant stream of frustrated, anxious, and annoyed people coming to my desk wanting "me first" treatment. I don't know where to start. The priorities are difficult to establish because they're always changing. More and more I find myself unable to manage all my co-workers' requests at the same time. Not only does my "To Do" list keep growing and changing from day to day, but people blame me for not getting to their priority first. I have a nervous stomach. Lately I've lost my appetite, which is lucky because I don't have time to eat anyway. Recently I've begun to bite my nails.

My boss is supposed to have the final decision over my priorities, but I have more than one boss. Each makes demands on me without realizing what the needs of the others are. I'm tense all the time and feel wired, like I'm stretched too tight. I never seem to fulfill my goals for the day. Since there's no hope to finish what I start, I feel disorganized and lost. I'm constantly second-guessing everything I do. Lately, I've begun referring to myself as "Airhead." How can I get some breathing room without getting everyone mad at me?

How to Set Priorities Without Losing Friends

Dear Airhead,

You are caught up in the tumultuous priorities game. It starts with one top priority, replaced by another and another ad infinitum. No matter how much you wish you could handle three top priorities at once, there can be only one priority at a time. The definition of a priority includes "precedence in time, order, and importance"—so says Webster's Dictionary. When everything is labeled a priority, all semblance of order is lost. The concept becomes meaningless. No wonder you feel disorganized. Rush job supersedes rush job, and the music goes round and round, ending in chaos. Our research reveals that most employees like to structure their work-days into a logical and consistent form.

Priorities that change constantly throw schedules off and wreak havoc with the best-laid plans. Stress increases because any sense of control over the work is often eliminated. You have to take control of setting priorities from your Pleaser.

There are some Pleaser stressful perceptions that keep you from doing this:

- If you make a priority decision, someone's feelings will be hurt.
- Every priority request must be accommodated.
- If you ask for help, you'll be bothersome.

A new perception to help you establish priorities with ease is that the more important items come first. People who are bumped down the priority list can deal with it. They are not as fragile as Pleaser thinks they are. Another realization is that requests can be accommodated by people other than yourself, and it's a sign of strength to ask for help. Asking for help is part of your job, not a sign that you are a bothersome pest.

Make the problem visible.

List each new job you get on a white board or flip chart in the order it comes. Be sure it's visible to those requesting "me first" treatment. When a frantic demand comes to "drop everything you're doing and get to this immediately," point to the board and show the requester what's already on your plate. If the person insists his or her work move to the top of the list, be pleasant but clear, and request that she or he negotiate this with the other managers. This is a very effective strategy. It has the added advantage of being nonthreatening, which makes your Pleaser feel safer. You don't have to speak up and confront. Let the white board do it for you.

Let the managers solve the priorities question.

Even if you think it will disturb the managers, you have to surface the issue by speaking up. Your managers are letting you decide which priorities take precedence. Then whatever you decide leaves you open to criticism. This is a no-win position. Your Pleaser is causing you to hide the fact that conflicting managerial priorities are hampering your efficiency. When you surface the problem, it becomes an issue for the managers to deal with, not just you. Managers get paid more to solve such problems, and many welcome the challenge.

Stress Tips Summary

Airhead doesn't do anyone a favor by self-sacrificing. Everyone thinks their priority is a 911 emergency. There's no need to come off as a grouch when people have to be told to wait. Her natural Pleaser compassion will soothe the frantic pleading of colleagues. It's perfectly all right to commiserate and say, "I understand how important this is to you and wish I could accommodate you, but I can't." Then it's immediately back to the stress tips, and she points to the white board. A good line is, "I'll get to this just as soon as I can. Count on it. But it won't hurt my feelings one bit if you can find someone else who can take care of it sooner."

TOPIC SUMMARY

Pleaser and Priority Stress

Dear Readers,

Speaking up and making problems visible is not easy in Pleaser mode. Along with reluctance to disappoint people is a common faulty perception that assertiveness will get you in trouble. It's essential that you point out what the snag is for everyone's benefit. By pointing out the need for help, managers will know you're overloaded even if they don't bring in a new hire. If management chooses to ignore the overload, they are making a conscious decision to let a serious systemic drag on the work flow continue.

The following is the advice of an administrator who used the white board strategy to solve her priority troubles: "The first thing I noticed was that the managers were amazed at how many assignments I had on the white board. No one had any idea I was being given so many jobs. Priorities in our department change rapidly. One manager was about to give me a new task. She saw the top priority I was about to start on was one she had previously assigned and realized that indeed it was more important than her new priority. She reestablished it as number one, and I didn't have to say a word."

In most workplaces the pace and flow of work are hectic and hurried. Everyone wants their needs met *now*. Setting priorities sometimes becomes a contest or test of wills. But it's impossible for everyone to get what they want in the time frame they demand. Strong, assertive personalities are usually too much for Pleaser to handle. So the first reaction is to give in. But if you're going to survive and retain some semblance of order and sanity, you've got to be firm. Pushy colleagues are under pressure themselves, and if they can catch you up in their anxiety, they've "gotcha!"

You will inevitably disappoint some people, and that has to be OK. The stronger and more assertive you are, the more others will respect you. Instead of demands, they will begin making "requests." That's what you want. You can help others by working with them to prioritize instead of letting them trample you.

When you begin to stand up for yourself, resist demanding colleagues, and become more assertive, conflict is inevitable. But you can and must learn to handle it. Pleaser's fear of and distaste for conflict is discussed in the next topic.

STRESSOR TOPIC

HOW TO TAME A REBELLIOUS SUBORDINATE

Many managers avoid or refuse to deal with conflict because of their Pleaser distaste for acrimony. The reasons are usually fear of causing antagonism and more headaches. When managers avoid conflict, it often has a ripple effect. Staff get upset because the boss is reluctant to deal with an employee who's causing discord. Everyone is irritated at the co-worker and even more disenchanted with their manager for not doing anything.

Pleaser effectively throttles any impulse the manager might have to confront a festering conflict. When the issue is finally laid on the table, the manager has to deal with an irate subordinate who is surprised that anything is amiss.

In the next letter, a manager's conflict phobia rankles the ranks. She succeeds in getting everybody mad at her—the very response she was trying to avoid.

The Insubordinate Subordinate

Dear Mary and Rene,

I am the project manager of a group on a critical assignment that is short-handed. Because of staff reductions and no new hires, it is essential that we all work together. One member of the team refuses to work with our group or the other groups who depend on our data. She's very efficient but only cares about her own duties. When confronted, she complains about her freedom being stifled and refuses to do anything but what she wants to do.

Unfortunately, she has a history of getting her way. In our meetings she resists me and raises objections to my plans for the group. Frequently she tries to play on my sympathies or make me feel remorseful by mentioning she was raised in a foster home. My other staff complain and pressure me to do something about her. I know how frustrating this is for them, so I listen sympathetically to their complaints. I tried asking the manager of the other group to speak to her, since he and his people are also complaining, but he didn't want to get involved. Nothing I do seems to work.

I'm upset most of the time, but usually avoid confronting her in the hope she will see the error of her ways and cooperate. I feel helpless and guilty because I'm letting everybody down. How do I get this subordinate to be a team player?

Conflict Phobia Rankles the Ranks

Dear Helpless and Guilty,

It's hard to understand what you're feeling guilty about. You are bending over backwards to be nice, which is the crux of the matter. Besides, nobody can *make* you feel guilty. Your Pleaser does that for you. Trying to smooth the ruffled feathers of your staff by listening to their gripes is a Pleaser attempt to solve the issue and relieve the guilt. This will make your Pleaser feel better but do nothing for the conflict. It only helps the other staff release their anger at the insubordinate subordinate by dumping it on you.

In this job war, the subordinate displays elements of two Stress Personalities. Her obstinate refusal to be a team player is Sabertooth. However, she also uses Inner Con Artist techniques—the "foster home gambit" and her "freedom fight"—to make her an even more formidable opponent. Against this combo your Pleaser is overmatched.

Other Pleaser behaviors that make it difficult to manage conflict are:

- Trying to be persistent but giving up because the other person gets angry and upset
- Attempting to persuade, reason, and cajole instead of making demands
- Avoiding confrontation whenever possible

Pleaser wants people to think well of you because if they do, they'll be reasonable and won't have to be confronted. So you give in rather than have someone get mad at you. But since everyone's ticked off anyway, a new approach is in order. View this from a different perception: When you deal assertively with this employee, the staff will appreciate and respect you for it. You will also respect yourself. From this perception the stress tips will be easier to put into practice.

Lay out clear performance expectations and document if they are not met.

When she refuses to meet performance expectations, you have grounds for disciplinary action. Include in the session a statement of what your expectations are and the sanction to be applied if she fails to cooperate. Do it in a one-to-one session. This is important when dealing with Sabertooth behavior. She won't feel exposed and will be less defensive. Dealing with Sabertooth requires firmness. Flatly assert your prerogatives as her supervisor. Impress on her that she must work with the team. And if this doesn't fit her career path, perhaps she'll need to look elsewhere. Most of the time when Sabertooth behavior is confronted firmly and directly, the person falls into line. The nicer and more reasonable you are, the less chance you have of succeeding. Since she is efficient at what she does, your Pleaser will feel better if you throw in some words of praise for good work. But stand firm.

Focus on the performance itself and do not accept excuses as they are nonapplicable.

Getting into a discussion with her about freedom is a total waste of time. It's basically the same thing as listening to her story about the foster home. Tell her it has no relevance to the basic issue, which is for her to follow your directives. Since Pleaser tends to personalize, stay away from personal stuff. Sidetracking you with stories of her sad childhood is an Inner Con Artist maneuver to gain your sympathy. Pleaser easily feels sorry for people and carries a burden of guilt for the sins of the world. Pity makes others seem less threatening. But it also puts you in a powerless position. Your Pleaser thinks it's cruel to take advantage of the pitiful. So you listen sympathetically and do nothing.

Bring the subordinate into more involvement with the group.

Don't let her remain isolated. When everyone gets upset and ignores her, they are playing into her hands. She wants to be left alone, so you are all accommodating her. Get her involved in working with others. Give her joint assignments with co-workers. Make sure everyone knows that you want this type of intermingling and see that it takes place. Peer pressure is an effective way to handle Con Artist behavior. Urge the other staff to tell her how they feel instead of running to you. Also, let the other manager know you need his cooperation. Conflict gets resolved when you actually face and deal with it. It's not as hard as you think.

Stress Tips Summary

Once free of conflict phobia, Helpless will be amazed at the positive effects of these stress tips. Her staff will be relieved and quit griping. The insubordinate subordinate will be required to become a part of the group with new responsibilities. Once the subordinate receives a firm statement of purpose, and if she chooses to stay and cooperate, all that energy she's been putting into resistance will be redirected. This means she can devote her full attention to her work instead of rebelling. And as a manager, Helpless will have handled a nettlesome conflict.

TOPIC SUMMARY

Conflict Phobia

Dear Readers,

Handling conflict requires assertiveness. But just what is meant by that term, and how is it affected by Pleaser? Several years ago we were doing a stress management workshop for a group of nurses, a high-Pleaser-content profession. One nurse took exception to our suggestion that assertiveness training was a good way to overcome Pleaser. "I took assertiveness training twice," she exclaimed. "It doesn't work." When we asked why, she replied, "I went home and tried it on my husband, and he told me to 'knock that crap off.'" The nurse looked around the room bewildered at the peals of laughter from her peers. She didn't get the joke.

Just as no one can "make" you feel guilty, no one "lets" you be assertive. This idea that other people are in charge of your feelings leads to the Pleaser sense of helplessness and victimization. Assertiveness, as opposed to aggressiveness, has more to do with standing up for your rights than dominating others by force. Pleaser misreads assertiveness as aggressiveness and so shies away from it. The reason we talk about not personalizing conflict interactions is that assertiveness is about solving issues, not massaging feelings.

Practice assertiveness in dealing with issues instead of bogging down in discussions of feelings. It's an important step in overcoming Pleaser's hold. Less personalizing is not the best course of action for every Stress Personality. For Striver, assertiveness comes naturally, and growth is in learning to pay more attention to people's feelings, not just the outcome of the interaction. For Pleaser, it's the opposite. More of the objectivity that comes so easily to Striver is needed.

Learning to set limits and say no when necessary is an assertive act. One of the major causes of Pleaser stress is the fear of saying no because of the guilt factor. If you've had little success in using the dreaded N word, you probably don't have enough skills to practice this important workplace necessity. The next topic explores some acceptable ways for Pleaser to say no without guilt.

STRESSOR TOPIC

A WAY TO SAY NO TO IMPOSSIBLE DEMANDS

Pleaser puts you in an untenable position. If you say yes to unreasonable demands, you feel used and angry. If you say no you feel guilty. To avoid the stress of guilt, you agree to the unreasonable demands. Pleaser uses guilt as blackmail to keep you doing the behaviors considered necessary for your survival. As the saying goes, guilt is the gift that keeps on giving.

So you will keep on giving as long as you feel remorseful. The key is to learn how to say no when necessary, and to reject the guilt sure to follow. In the next case, fear of saying no to impossible demands threatens to turn an accommodating support engineer into a basket case.

Support Engineer Tilts at Windmills

Dear Mary and Rene,

Being a resource to the sales force, I'm often overscheduled and over-booked. I can't say no when asked to do something. I feel caught in an impossible dream where everyone is crazily tilting at windmills like Don Quixote. To my knowledge no one in sales is crazy, like this literary figure, but they have ridiculous goals and expectations for the support staff. I'm like Quixote's sidekick Sancho. I try to help sales fight their windmills.

In the last six months we've downsized from twelve people to five, but we're expected to provide more support than when we were at full staffing. As part of sales support I'm supposed to commit "lots" of time to win the business. But since I have so many reps to support, I don't have the time to give them. I feel bad turning anyone down, so I commit, even though I know I can't always follow through. I try to be rational and tell myself I must accept the projects because it's my job and I have no choice.

Work has become drudgery and isn't fun anymore. I've become less receptive and enthusiastic about my job. I feel nervous, guilty, and tense, and it shows up at home. How can I get these people to realize I can't do it all? I believe the more I do and the more I try to make others happy, the better person/employee I am. I suspect this is BS. What do you think?

Don Quixote and the Impossible Sales Dream

Dear Sancho,

Your better judgment has given you the answer to your last question, which is yes. Your quality as a good person or employee has nothing to do with how happy other people are. Your competence and their happiness are not linked.

Pleaser will have you believe that if you tell people the truth, they will be unhappy, which makes you a bad employee/person. A new perception is that it's your duty to be up front. It's best for people to know you're doing all you can under the circumstances. Then they can either accept the fact that they have to wait for service or look at other options for getting help sooner.

Here are some of the Pleaser beliefs that keep you in the impossible dream:

- Others should realize how busy you are and be reasonable.
- If you tell people what they want to hear, they'll like you.
- If you say no to anyone, you are not a team player.

The fable of Don Quixote is an apt allegory for your predicament. Accompanied by his faithful manservant Sancho Panza, Don Quixote roamed the countryside attacking windmills with his lance under the delusion that they were giants. To tilt at windmills means to pursue a course doomed to frustration. Your sidekick, Pleaser, is like Sancho Panza was with Don Quixote: your partner in trying to slay the sales windmills. Like Sancho, who couldn't bring himself to tell Don Quixote the truth about his futile crusade, you're not willing to tell sales the truth about your impossible work load.

Successful salespeople are often aggressive and demanding, and Pleaser is easily intimidated. In order to avoid saying no, Pleaser hopes that others will recognize how busy you are, take pity, and back off. Then you won't have to be the bad guy setting limits on their demands. It's an impossible dream because it's not going to happen. There's no way you're going to get them to realize that you can't do it all. They want what they want when they want it. You're the one who has to stop fighting windmills and decide when you are too busy to take on more. Because you won't say no when needed, you're increasing the pressure on yourself. Pleaser's anguish comes from the belief that you're failing sales by not accomplishing the impossible.

To avoid the inevitable frustration of impossible demands, get your Pleaser under control with the following stress tips.

To set limits on demands, avoid the automatic yes.

Start cutting back on saying yes by building in some time to think about whether you can really do what's demanded of you. It's a Pleaser characteristic to say yes reflexively. Then, after succumbing, you feel mortified that you took on still another job you can't get to. Delay your answer by creating some time to think before you respond. For instance, you can say, "Let me check my schedule and get back to you." This gives you time to evaluate the request. It also gives the demanders an option to find another way to get the job done if they are in a hurry.

Develop a new perception that it's also your job to help others help themselves.

Many support professionals have learned how to redirect some of the tasks they are asked to do, rather than doing everything themselves. The reality is that downsizing affects everybody, not just you. The quality of the service is not going to be the same. Sales has to come to grips with the fact that there are now five of you doing the work of twelve. You can become a guide and show people how to accomplish things. This saves time for everybody. Rein-terpret this as part of your service. If a task can be done just as easily by someone else, guide them through the steps so that next time they can do it on their own. Ask yourself what you can teach sales representatives about your job so that they can be more independent.

Stress Tips Summary

Other people in Sancho's position have discovered how to set limits on their Pleasers to reduce stress and increase productivity. Here are a couple of their tips:

- "I've learned to ask for managerial assistance in scheduling new work. It's easier for me to say, 'My manager says I don't have time,' than for my Pleaser to say no."

  —Administrator

- "It's been important for me to practice saying no as often as I can. I found it's a skill one has to learn in order to be effective. I'm finding ways that are comfortable for me and acceptable to others. Even so, I still say yes more than I should."

  —Support Engineer

TOPIC SUMMARY

No Is Not a Four-Letter Word

Dear Readers,

Pleaser is the Stress Personality that has the most difficulty saying no. Everyone in corporate life has to set limits on themselves and how much they can do. In the Pleaser belief system, if you take care of yourself you are selfish. Therefore you must be hurting someone else. This eternal self-sacrifice has a backlash. As you get overwhelmed and less productive, the stress builds in the form of resentment and frustration, and you feel victimized. This can lead to a Sabertooth outburst, despondency, burnout and a desire to quit your job.

Many of you will say, "Yes, but in our company you can never say no lest you be hung with the dreaded label, 'Not a team player.'" This epithet causes great apprehension for your Pleaser. The ability to set limits by saying no does not mean you aren't a cooperative member of the team. We've seen countless examples of people who've been inundated with so much work because they can't say no that they have become inefficient, with zero productivity. That's not being a good team player.

When you say yes to everything, you're misleading people into thinking you can actually do it all. It raises unrealistic expectations in others, and then they get angry with you when you can't deliver. Pleaser feels guilty and bad and blurts out another rash promise to make up for disappointing someone. Most of your colleagues already know how many times you'll say no before they can get a yes out of you. When you realize you can't accomplish something, push back and say so.

In every workshop we do there is a discussion between those comfortable with saying no, and those who aren't. The Pleaser fear usually expressed is that "saying no will get you fired." Our question is why would they fire someone who is doing the job of two or three people. Those comfortable with saying no have often overcome their Pleaser fear and found to their surprise that standing up for themselves is not fatal. In fact, it improves work relationships, and most find their productivity increases. Also bear in mind that there are millions of successful, highly respected people in companies who know how to say no and do so when necessary.

POSTSCRIPT

Martyrdom Can Be Hazardous to Your Health

Dear Readers,

Pleaser is like the perennial jilted lover left at the altar, always waiting for someone to show up and make everything all right. If you are waiting for your company to take care of you, forget it. You work for an organization whose purpose is to produce things. The goal is to get as much production out of each worker as possible. Pleaser laments, "I give so much, I should get something back." That "something back" is, "My company will look after my best interests in return."

Typical questions we get asked reflect a concern about how the corporate powers view the plight of their employees. "Can't they see how overworked we are?" "Do they care about the stress we're under?" "Do you tell them what's going on?" After many years of hearing these questions and trying to act on the concerns voiced, we've discovered the answer. There is no "they." This will come as bad news to your Pleaser. Your company is an entity, not a parent or loving relative. Downsizing and reorganization mean the "they" constantly change. Companies become huge and bureaucratic, and authority is diffused. There is no "they" there.

The reason we emphasize that you must take care of yourself is that nobody else is going to. Your organization will use you as much as you allow yourself to be used. It's nothing personal. Nobody is bad. Your boss isn't bad. Your company isn't bad. Capitalism isn't bad. You are a commodity and your work is important. But you have to take care of yourself or you become damaged goods.

When you allow yourself to be overwhelmed with work and then feel bad when someone "up there" doesn't notice, you are not taking care of yourself. There is nothing selfish about looking after your own best interests. In fact, it's smart. If you work yourself into so much stress that your health is seriously impaired, you will be a less valuable commodity. If you burn out, you will be replaced, and that's expensive for both you and your company. So it's in the best interests of both you and your employer for you to stay healthy and in charge of your career.

In our workshops we have been astounded by the number of reported health problems from workplace stress. These run from the fairly serious to the really serious. More than once we've been told by participants of our programs that they were so dedicated to their jobs they worked while ill to the point of collapse. Then they had to be carried from their workstation on a stretcher and whisked away in an ambulance. Is this dedication or foolhardiness?

A surprisingly large number of people never take vacations, even though they have them coming. One employee told us he had not had a vacation for twelve years. He had been sent to the workshop by his doctor because he failed a treadmill test and was having chest pains. His reason for not taking a vacation? He was told that there was no backup for his position, therefore he was indispensable. The question he struggled with was, "If I'm the only person who knows how to do this job in a company of several thousand employees, is this my personal concern, or is it an organizational defect?" Up to that time, his Pleaser had prevented him from popping that question.

Another person lamented that she had to work every holiday including Thanksgiving and Christmas for six years, because nobody else wanted to. Her manager told her how much he appreciated it and said to her, "Thank you for doing this. It makes it so much easier for everyone." She complained in the workshop of being chronically exhausted and didn't know why.

The single most stressful Pleaser trait is the belief that you must make everyone happy at all times under every circumstance. It causes employees to plod through their work life at a pace of 50 to 60 hours a week and never say no to anybody. Despite this, there's always someone who's unhappy, and this self-imposed stressor leaves you unhappiest of all.

Our research is filled with the Pleaser faulty perception that you must keep everyone else happy, even at the expense of your own happiness and health. This belief causes more work, grief, stress, and wasted energy than anyone needs. One important step in taking charge of Pleaser is to move the focus off pleasing others and please yourself more often.

Pleaser is too other-directed. Pleasing yourself will bring you back into a healthy balance. Trying to please everyone all the time and make them happy is a futile effort, every bit as much as Don Quixote's tilting at windmill giants. Since this is impossible to achieve, you need to move to what is possible. Figure out what you need to do to limit your work overload and make it more manageable. You have to control Pleaser on the job or you will continue to be eaten alive.

The stress tips in this chapter illustrate ways to modify Pleaser, look after your own best interest, and do a good job. In this chapter we've discussed four of the highest-stress situations reported that trigger Pleaser stress: unreasonable expectations and demands, constantly changing priorities, interpersonal conflict, and the inability to say no. All require the skills of setting limits and learning that no is not a four-letter word.

QUICK-REFERENCE STRESS TIPS FOR *PLEASER*

We suggest you take one of these tips every day, write it down or tear it out of this book, and refer to it all day long. This will give you practice thinking and acting more assertively .

- Be persistent in going after what you want.
- Let people know what you're thinking; don't expect them to guess.
- Stand up for yourself.
- Be direct.
- Do one thing for yourself each week.
- Confront conflicts early on.
- Express yourself when others upset you or when you disagree with them.
- Make problems visible.
- Define help as helping others to help themselves.
- Set limits on demands.
- Find a way to say no and mean it.

CHAPTER 3

Striver

Roadblocks on the Fast Track

How to Recognize *Striver*

Kelly throws up her hands. Another frustrating meeting with her manager. She just can't seem to impress upon him the need for additional resources to complete the project she heads. She's indignant. Chosen to create "the" product that could propel the company to another plateau, she's been put under the thumb of inept management with no vision. She knows that without adequate resources and total commitment the deadline will slip.

She chafes under a decision-making procedure fraught with barriers, obstacles, and general inertia. The dithering, debate, and overanalysis baffle and agitate her. As the project completion cycle approaches, the group isn't making any progress. No one else seems to understand how to build a product. Others don't appreciate the complexity and extra effort involved. Kelly is irate and exasperated at not getting the proper recognition for her well planned and executed efforts.

An additional frustration is that despite all her hard work, there's the looming possibility that the project she is giving her all for might end up in a box. A sense of creeping despondency and helplessness are beginning to dampen the fire in her belly.

These feelings are highly contradictory to the way she normally sees her creative, energetic nature. She's caught herself complaining, which she disparages in others as "sniveling." At the end of the day she's physically and emotionally depleted. Kelly knows she's working too hard in what seems like a futile effort. Lately, she's been thinking about quitting to search for a group that could better use her talents. Her never-ending quest for high achievement, recognition, and perfection indicate that Kelly's Striver is dominating her life.

THE *STRIVER* STRESS TEST

Read the questions below and place a check (✔) in the appropriate column to the right to indicate your response. Find out how your Striver beliefs and behaviors increase your stress. Pay attention to the questions you checked "Usually" and "Frequently." These have to be reduced to "Occasionally" or "Seldom" in order to control Striver.	NEVER	SELDOM	OCCASIONALLY	FREQUENTLY	USUALLY
Do I: 1. Assume anything can be achieved if I work hard enough? 2. Take on more than I can handle? 3. Behave competitively at work, home, and play? 4. Get labeled a workaholic by family and friends? 5. Have to be the best to be satisfied with my job? 6. Expect others to live up to my expectations? 7. Lose motivation when my work is not appreciated? 8. Become bored and disengaged when I don't get my way? 9. Feel frustrated and apathetic when not promoted fast enough? 10. Experience chronic job dissatisfaction?					

How *Striver* Causes Stress

Striver is difficult to rein in. The all-consuming nature of this high flyer is stimulated by a restless excitement that can be addictive. Those adrenaline rushes you get when everything is going your way, and you're humming along at optimal efficiency, are continually sought after. The downside? When not high on achieving you're low, bored, or depressed. This seesaw of high and low is Striver stress.

Because this Stress Personality expects you to meet every challenge regardless of the circumstances, you overextend yourself. You take on two or three jobs at once. You've bought into the Striver belief that if you try hard enough you can accomplish anything. But the heavy load takes its toll. You can't even manage to get the work out, let alone meet Striver's expectations of excellence. When you feel overwhelmed and realize your quality is slipping, job satisfaction evaporates.

Advice to the Job Stressed

In the next section of "Roadblocks on the Fast Track," job stressors that trip up Striver on the ladder of success are examined. How to balance ambition with opportunity and Striver's propensity to grab it all is the subject of "Opportunity Knocks on the Wrong Door." Using discretion while working toward career goals points the way to less stress, and ambition is still rewarded.

The subject of health and workaholism is discussed in "American Karoshi." Addiction to work means losing sight of all other aspects of life. The stress tips suggest how to create balance and fulfillment.

The next Striver Advice example deals with unrealistic expectations. In "Perfectionist Downsized," perfectionism is seen as a Striver flaw in today's "hurry up" workplace. A new definition of perfection is to readjust expectations to what is possible under difficult circumstances.

In "Firefighter Gets Burned," an up-and-coming Striver seeks visibility and advancement. But his career goals are compromised because he's fighting the fires of others all day long and can't meet his own goals. He learns that it's possible to meet the challenges necessary for his advancement and juggle the emergencies of others.

Read the "Dear Mary and Rene" letters. The replies to these letters show you how to reduce the stress of Striver's relentless pressure.

STRESSOR TOPIC

HOW TO CHOOSE THE RIGHT OPPORTUNITY

Striver never met an opportunity it didn't like or could let pass. Taking advantage of an opportunity involves selecting the right one at the right time. When every opportunity seems too enticing to pass up, the selectivity factor is lost. Better ones come along and you're too bogged down to avail yourself of them. Furthermore, chasing workplace rainbows leads to grueling hours in search of that elusive pot of gold called success.

The following letter illustrates how overheated ambition leads to a dead end of endless toil and no satisfaction.

Opportunity Knocks on the Wrong Door

Dear Mary and Rene,

Nine months ago, I was offered an opportunity that looked so good I couldn't pass it up. A management position became available because the previous manager left. The assignment did not come with title or money, but it came with all the responsibilities. To learn the job, and to get the project to where it is today, I worked your basic eighty-hour week for six months. Finally, I've gotten my head above water and my hours down to fifty. Now my manager wants to offer another new opportunity because he says I'm so competent. This one doesn't come with title or additional salary either.

It's hard to let this opportunity slip through my fingers, but I'm concerned about getting in over my head. As it is, I keep getting assigned more projects on top of those I already have because I do my work "so well." The real killer is that I'm the lowest-ranked person in my peer group while carrying the highest work load and productivity expectations. Although my manager has hinted repeatedly that I'll be officially promoted, nothing has been promised.

Recently, I've noticed my interest in the success of the projects fluctuates. I'm beginning to procrastinate and avoid my manager's invitation to "project talk." I work longer hours but don't get much done. I'm having a repeated anxiety dream about flunking out of school even though I graduated years ago. I wake up feeling alarmed. I'm really uptight and overwrought. I want to get ahead, but the question is, how do I get ahead without so much stress?

Burning Ambition Backfires

Dear Uptight and Overwrought,

Ambition without discretion is a frustrating path to nowhere. Striver will push you until you fail if you let it. This Stress Personality operates on a personal Peter Principle: As you take on more, you eventually reach the point where competency falls off. Then it's a struggle just to keep your head above water. Eighty hours a week is not a career, it's an obsession. You've been putting in more and more time doing a manager's job with no payoff. Your reward is more work. It's no wonder this is a "killer" for you, but ask yourself who really is responsible. Your Striver is an eager accomplice with your boss and the only one you have control over. It's not surprising you're having anxiety dreams. They reflect the intense pressure you're putting on yourself.

Striver hunger to get ahead leads to the following stressful traits. Ask yourself if you:

■ Believe working long hours is a sure road to success

■ Dream of lofty rewards that entice you to overextend

■ Are convinced you should jump at every opportunity

A new perception that will help you sleep better at night is that life is full of opportunities, and the right ones will find you. Anxiety dreams are a subterranean message about your overheated aspirations. The scenario of a common Striver dream puts you back in college, just before graduation. Finals are looming, and you realize at the last minute that you forgot to attend one class and are sure to flunk. This dream is about thwarted ambition and work overload. These kind of dreams in general reflect an unconscious sense that your life is out of control. The following stress tips will help you use discretion and decide what you want.

Use discretion when offered opportunity.

 Harness Striver ambition to goals you've decided on. Say no to propositions that take you off track. Striver won't let you pass up any opportunity because it could be the "big one." This is the orgasmic theory of success. Entertain a new perception: Advancement is best guaranteed if you are picky. Enthusiastically endorse your manager's offers when they fit your career path. Say little about the ones that don't.

Carefully scrutinize promises of reward.

You're letting yourself get swept up by the Striver energy of your boss. He may well be trying to boost your career. But hints, although seductive, are not promises. You are being lured along by the carrot on the stick. Put pressure on him to expand on those hints. Ask for time lines as to when these rewards will materialize. Be persistent. He'll try to put you off as long as possible.

Decide what you want *now.*

Like many people these days, you seem to be longing for time, not just money. Decide whether time, home life, or money is most important. If it's money, divide your eighty-hour week and sleepless nights into your salary and compute what you're really earning. If you want more free time, limit the amount of hours you agree to. This will automatically limit the amount you take on.

Stress Tips Summary

When Overwrought realizes that ambition alone is not enough to ensure success, she will be able to focus on what she really wants. She can point herself toward clear goals instead of just accomplishing heroic output. By being more discerning she will have time for herself in her off hours and no longer be overwrought.

TOPIC SUMMARY

Ambition and Opportunity

Dear Readers,

Hunger for recognition propels Striver and can cloud your judgment. Any opportunity, real or imagined, represents potentially tantalizing prospects. Promises of promotion that don't materialize cause high achievers to feel betrayed and resentful at not receiving recognition for their super efforts. This challenges Striver's belief that going all out insures reward. Then follows the inevitable deflated enthusiasm and drive. Many of our program participants have fallen for this temptation only to be disappointed when the prize doesn't materialize as expected.

Added to the stress of the Striver struggle for recognition is the fact that downsizing in organizations has resulted in fewer chances for promotion. Recognition is available in the form of increased responsibility but not in the form of upward mobility. So people are given important assignments as a "reward" for their competency. These "rewards" often lead to frustrating dead-end experiences. This is when Striver takes a dive. Feeling stuck, with nowhere to climb, Striver loses self-esteem. To Striver, if you're not getting ahead, you're falling behind. Stress for Striver is often self-induced. Enough is never enough, and many people bite off more than they can chew healthily. When the burden gets to be too much it can have serious repercussions on your health.

STRESSOR TOPIC

RECOVERING FROM WORKAHOLISM

The term *workaholic* is in common usage. It's described in a variety of ways. Sometimes people attach a positive meaning and sometimes it's an epithet, as in, "You'd better watch it, you're a workaholic." The concept generally refers to someone who is addicted to work. There is an old aphorism, not at all accurate, that nobody ever died of too much work. In Japan, they've challenged that belief and even invented a name for death from overwork: *karoshi*. Whether Striver's influence on you is enough to be fatal is a question. It depends on how healthy you are and whether you are willing to scale back on your habit.

In the following example, a workaholic with high blood pressure voices concern about his health, and wonders if he's overdoing it. A heart attack suffered by a friend gets his attention, and he suspects that there is an American version of karoshi and that he is a prime candidate.

American Karoshi

Dear Mary and Rene,

I'm involved in a project that is understaffed and under the gun to perform more efficiently. We're working longer days and weekends. There is no funding for additional positions, which means there's no help in sight. Schedules are tight, and the project keeps growing in scope and complexity. The pressure is increasing because a competitor is coming out with a similar product and we're being exhorted to beat them to the market. I don't mind the grueling hours and the constant fatigue, but the stress of all this is affecting my health. I've been on medication for hypertension.

Sometimes I get dizzy. My blood pressure is up, and that's probably the cause. My doctor has warned me that this could have serious long-term consequences. Last month a former colleague at another company had a heart attack. He's my age, thirty-four, and this jolted me. We're very much alike, and our wives have accused us both of being workaholics. My wife often calls me at work to find out when I'll be leaving as she's concerned that I stay too long. Recently she gave me an article about the Japanese death-from-overwork phenomenon called "karoshi." Is there an American version of karoshi, what is its name, and how do I tell if I've got it?

The High Price of *Striveroshi*

Dear Karoshi,

Nobody that we know of has coined a similar term in this country yet. However, workaholic is pretty close. How about Striveroshi? This Stress Personality is merciless and will push you without regard for health consequences. If you were to have a dialogue with your Striver and ask the question, "Do you care about my health?" the answer you'd get is, "Of course, because you have to stay healthy to perform." But if good health has to be sacrificed for success, Striver will say, "That's the price you have to pay." In essence, there is a price on your head as far as Striver is concerned. Striver's mission is to keep your nose to the grindstone at all costs.

If you're wondering how much you are afflicted with Striveroshi, check out these traits of workaholism: Do you

- Ignore warning signs of illness because they're inconvenient?
- Keep working even when exhausted?
- Usually work later than you intended?

It's a good sign that you're inquiring about karoshi. Your workaholic friend may have ignored the signs along the way, but it appears you aren't making the same mistake. Sounds like both wives had you two pegged. Striver gets so wound up in the job that even though you sense you need to pay more attention to your health, this slave driver won't give you the time. "Not right now," says Striver. "Later will be better." Later often comes too late.

Pay attention to how many times your wife calls you at the office late in the evening to encourage you to come home. You put her off with the comment, "I just want to finish this one more item, and I'll be right there." Several hours later you notice you're still working even though you feel exhausted. Both your wife's phone call and the daily fatigue are indications of your workaholism. Counter Striver's argument to push on to completion no matter what with a new perception: "I will do a better job when I'm rested."

The following Stress Tips will instruct your Samurai on healthier living.

STRESS TIPS   A HEALTHY SAMURAI

Broaden the definition of success.

Success is a subjective measurement, with many possible meanings. Striver needs a broader definition to include a balanced life. Success can also mean being a good parent, a loving and attentive spouse, a solid friend who's there when needed. It can also be defined as one who leads a fulfilled life. Enjoy your family and friends. Make time for them. Take a vacation once in a while. It puts another spin on life. To bring Striver to heel, imagine the inscription on your gravestone after you've died from *Striver-oshi*: "Here lies a good worker. He never missed a deadline." The following quotation with a similar thought comes from a reader of our *Advice to the Job Stressed* newsletter. Hanging on the wall of his computer room at home is an old saying his wife hung up years ago that reads as follows: "No one ever wished on their deathbed that they'd spent more time at the office."

Postpone tasks that can wait, but give yourself reminders.

One good suggestion from someone who says he's "been there and done that" is to send yourself some e-mail at the end of the day listing the remaining tasks and open issues to be resolved. They will greet you the next day as the first item. We suggest that you tell Striver that you'll meet again in the morning, close the door on this Stress Personality, and go home before your wife has to call again.

Pay close attention to your health during high stress situations.

Your body knows when it's being overtaxed and warns you with symptoms. Pay attention to these signals. If you ignore them your body has no way to stay in touch with you about your health. This communication breakdown can be fatal. Monitor your blood pressure and note when it rises. By establishing a pattern of when the spike occurs, you can predict what's going to set you off

and can plan accordingly. A key to handling a Stress Personality is to be aware of when it's influencing you. With time, you will be able to reduce stressful reactions by knowing which situations you're most vulnerable to. Then keep Striver out in these pressure-packed stress conditions.

Stress Tips Summary

When Karoshi begins to recognize the symptoms of too much work and predict which types of Striver pressures are most likely to push his buttons, he'll be prepared in advance for the stress assault. A study done for the Army by the National Science Foundation found that the best stress management techniques are those that allow one to predict high-stress situations in advance and prepare for them, whether on the battlefield or in the office. Stress Personalities are an effective predictive tool. These tips will help get Karoshi out of the narrow existence of workaholism, reintroduce him to family life, and actually increase his efficiency.

TOPIC SUMMARY

Life Is Short; Make It Sweet

Dear Readers,

People continually jeopardize their health by working too much, letting go of exercise and quality time with their families. If you identify with *Striver*oshi, give up the notion that being called a workaholic is a compliment. Many work nuts love to show others the nobility of suffering through staggering work loads. One manager liked to call his staff at home in the middle of the night ostensibly to ask questions but really to make sure everyone knew he was toiling around the clock. In many companies they play the "parking lot visibility game." People stay late and peek out the window to notice whose cars are still in the parking lot. Presumably, the later you leave the more valuable you are. Work nuts have even been known to get married on their lunch hour in the company parking lot, and then it's back to work they go.

It's an old saying that there is more to life than work. Yet many ignore this under the influence of Striver. A study by the Palo Alto Consulting Center, a division of the Tom Peters Group, polled male business executives. Among the findings: "Sixty-eight percent of senior executives said that they had neglected their family lives to pursue professional goals. Half said they would spend less time working and more time with their wives and children if they could start over again." But of course they can't. Many senior citizens we've interviewed said, "I've never looked back and regretted the fact that I didn't work enough. What I wish is that I'd taken more time to travel and develop other interests in life."

There is nothing inherently stressful in work itself. As we say in karoshi, the stress comes from the driven need to find all your satisfaction in this one arena. The phrase "don't work harder, work smarter" also applies to Stress Personalities. If you maintain executive control over Striver, you can avoid *Striver*oshi and not work yourself to death.

One way people cause themselves stress and longer hours is a Striver obsession with trying to be perfect even in imperfect conditions.

STRESSOR TOPIC

THE STRESS OF TRYING TO BE PERFECT

In the previous chapter, we mentioned the unrealistic expectations of Pleaser in trying to make everyone happy all the time. An unrealistic expectation of Striver is the self-imposed need for perfection. It's tied to the idea that only the best will do all the time. This stressful perception is also imposed on others who fail to do what you want them to do. If you require meticulous attention to every detail, and your performance expectations demand perfection, you're making life tougher on yourself than it need be. Others dragged into your system of belief will inevitably fail you. They may not be able or willing to see the brilliant clarity of your reasoning and are satisfied with their own way of doing things.

In the next Advice case, a downsized perfectionist insists on impeccable performance from himself and everyone else. Much to his dismay, others don't share his vision of excellence.

Perfectionist Downsized

Dear Mary and Rene,

Since the last downsizing we have tripled the amount of work. Our group had five people; now there are just two of us left, my manager and I. Both of us expect me to fill the shoes of five. Because I'm a perfectionist, everything I do has to be done flawlessly. I'm concerned that I won't be able to keep up my high standards. I'm constantly frustrated at not being able to do my best.

To complicate matters, my work depends on receiving data from others. These colleagues rarely give me the quality information I need.

I've sent them memos outlining the specifications needed, but I usually have to rework their data, which puts me even farther behind. I've been coming to work on weekends to get everything done but still can't get caught up. I feel annoyed and somewhat embarrassed because I pride myself on a job well done. A further irritant is that I have a small ulcer, which I feel is quite ridiculous because I'm pretty young. How can a perfectionist gain satisfaction in a downsizing?

Trying to Be Perfect in a "Rightsized" World

Dear Perfectionist,

Your Striver has set you up for a stress overload by insisting on perfection even under the most difficult circumstances. Your description of yourself as a perfectionist is a tip-off that Striver expectations are causing you needless stress. A Striver stressful perception regarding this is that there is only one measure of quality that's acceptable, and it's the one Striver sets. Sometimes even you don't pass that test, and you feel bad. Others almost always fail, and you're disappointed. The stress comes from trying to live up to this phantom standard.

Here are examples of stressful perceptions that contribute to perfectionism:

- If you don't do something flawlessly you've failed.
- Colleagues should live up to your expectations.
- One person can do the work of five perfectly if they try hard enough.

You and your boss are both stuck in the Striver mode. Just because both of you want you to do the job of five doesn't mean it's possible to pull it off. Even your boss is more realistic than your Striver. He just wants you to do five jobs at once. It's you that have added the stressful qualification of perfection. This works fine until reality rears its ugly head and you hit the wall of unattainable demands. When you continue to expect that you must do the undoable, your stress level soars and your productivity drops.

A Word About Your Ulcers

New evidence points to bacteria as the cause of ulcers. This has led some to downplay the role of stress in their development. However, susceptibility to infection from bacteria increases under stress. A high-stress lifestyle over prolonged periods of time lowers the body's immune response, making you more vulnerable to microbes of all kinds. To feel irritated about yourself because you're too young to suffer such an imperfection only increases stress. It's caused by your Striver's disdain that your young body could suffer such a pedestrian ailment. To broaden Striver's tunnel vision, read the following stress tips.

STRESS TIPS   CURING EXPECTATION OVERBITE

Work toward perfection within limits.

Give Striver free rein within time constraints. A new perception to accomplish this is, "I can strive to be as perfect as I want within a time limit." Whatever is accomplished within the time frame is to be regarded as perfection. That way you will succeed by staying within the framework of your Striver's belief system but with an important stipulation: you keep the Striver goal but set realistic limits. This will satisfy your need to both strive and manage your stress. These dual desires will no longer be in conflict, and your stress level will even out.

Accept that others have different standards.

Get out of the habit of redoing other people's work. When you receive work you need from colleagues, ask yourself, "Is it good enough, even though it's not perfect?" Challenge your Striver to expand your options from perfection, which you'll seldom get, to "good enough," which you'll often get. No matter how much your Striver frets and fusses about others not satisfying your criteria, this paraphrase of a pearl of wisdom from Gestalt therapist Fritz Perls might help: Others aren't in this world to meet your expectations, nor are you here to meet theirs. If they should mesh, great; if not, don't get hung up on it.

Stress Tips Summary

Putting these stress tips into action will improve working relationships between Perfectionist and his colleagues. One of the major conflicts that shows up in our research is the Striver penchant for always changing work given to them in order to put their own stamp on it. It's like cougars marking their territory. Others are infuriated at always having their work tampered with. It comes across as arrogant and presumptuous. Once Perfectionist learns to take "good enough" and make use of it, he'll win friends and cut down the needless hours spent trying to satisfy his Striver.

Perfectionism as a Flaw

Dear Readers,

For those of you who identify yourselves as perfectionists, today's fast-paced work environment will frustrate you. Product has to be catapulted out the door and into the market quickly before someone beats you to the punch. Trying to be an exemplar of fastidiousness under these conditions is very stressful and is usually not appreciated. You could even be regarded as an impediment to progress.

Your job may not be the place to satisfy Striver's craving. You may need a place other than work in which you can give an activity the loving attention you desire. Apply that need to the home front. You could start a hobby where you set all the parameters and lavish as much attention on it as you wish. However, don't set the hobby standards so high that you take all the pleasure out of it. In sports—like golf, for instance—people can get so stressed over their game that it ceases to be recreation and becomes neurosis. Be sure you don't get carried away at a hobby with the usual Striver determination.

Letting go of perfectionism is a must if your job involves dealing with continual crisis. During such hectic times, quick fixes and fast action are often necessary. Your normal methodical attention to quality may not be possible. And you'll quite likely fail the stress test if you try to be perfect on the crisis treadmill, as the next topic discusses.

STRESSOR TOPIC

HOW TO MANEUVER ON THE CRISIS TREADMILL

The last topic we'll cover for Striver involves another unrealistic expectation: goal fixation. A handicap of Striver is a tendency to be too goal directed. Once the target is locked in, Striver must get you there. But what if the objectives lose their efficacy? Things change, and sometimes Striver has to have a bucket of cold water in the face to realize it. Achievements come in many guises, and Striver's periscope sometimes misses possible benefits within easy view. In the following letter, constant crisis wrecks the carefully laid plans of a methodical quality control auditor. He's not flexible enough to see the forest for the trees.

Firefighter Gets Burned

Dear Mary and Rene,

I make up my own priority list every day, and I feel good about it and in control of my schedule. I begin to work my way down the list in an orderly fashion. Before I know it, I'm hit with everybody's demands. I wind up firefighting all day long. What I had deemed important for myself, getting my own stuff done, gets pushed to the bottom of the pile. I still have to do it but can't because I'm strictly on react mode all day.

Not only do I have to handle never-ending crises, but even these have no order as one follows another in haphazard fashion. I'm evaluated on the work I'm supposed to do but can't get to. I need to be visible in the company so my achievements will be noticed. It's the only way to get ahead. But I'm buried under all this crisis and can't meet my own goals. When I can't finish what I start it seems like I'm on a treadmill and performing badly. I lose energy and am less responsive to what could be real emergencies. I'm short tempered and notice lately that I'm more aggressive. On some particularly trying days I get back spasms. Sometimes I'm so steamed that I feel like calling it a day and walking out. How do I fight fires and still meet my own goals?

Constant Emergencies Bury Job in Rubble

Dear Firefighter,

Sounds like your fire engine is overheating. Your Striver gets satisfaction when you accomplish what you set out to do. This part of you likes to set goals and meet them. As your day disintegrates, control is lost. When you keep getting hit with new demands all day, those sacrosanct goals you set in the morning are bushwhacked.

The feeling that you are helpless to stay on top of this disorder is the stress. Your desire for achievement is being thwarted. Because Striver wants to be in charge of everything, the react mode is particularly distressing. It feels like everyone else owns your time.

Other examples of Striver behaviors that keep you dissatisfied while in crisis mode include:

- Trying to control the uncontrollable
- Insisting that your job meet all your expectations
- Adhering rigidly to schedules when the job calls for flexibility

Question what your job really is. Is it to get through your priority projects or to help others? If you are being evaluated and judged by your ability to complete your own projects, you'd better get clear with your manager on this. If firefighting is your primary job, then juggling the emergencies of others is your priority. Don't accept the mixed message from your Striver that you can do both at the same time. Your Striver insists on clinging to the stressful perception that if you're organized enough you should be able to regulate all aspects of the day. When you focus on your untouched work and quest after the time to get to it but can't, you label yourself a poor performer. The labeling process adds to the stress because your Striver takes pride in top performance.

The following tips, once put in place, will help you find job satisfaction in what you're really doing, not just what you want to do.

STRESS TIPS   CRISIS—MOTHER OF CREATIVE FLEXIBILITY

Be flexible and adjust to variable demands.

Use all that Striver talent to figure out how to be a terrific and satisfied firefighter. Relabel disruptions as challenges instead of a series of impositions. Striver easily gets bored with repetition. You have an opportunity to fill your workday with examples of your problemsolving skill. By gaining the reputation as a hotshot crisis doctor you can attain success and visibility. Set your schedule so that you have flexibility to be creative. A new perception is that you are hired to work a certain amount of time to fix the problems that arise. Maybe that *is* your job.

Negotiate priorities.

If your boss says you have to be a firefighter and also do your assigned projects, negotiate this—especially if your manager is also pushed by Striver's unrealistic expectations. Perhaps you can stagger your work week. Monday, Wednesday, and Friday you fight fires. Tuesday and Thursday you work on your own stuff. With your manager, identify what your role really is, not what it's supposed to be. Help your boss recognize that some of the time you're a firefighter and some of the time you aren't. Plan uninterrupted time when you take off the fireman's hat and complete your other duties. That way you'll be successful on all your workdays. Striver will love that.

Stress Tips Summary

When Firefighter learns to recognize crisis management as a valuable skill, he'll realize that it can provide the visibility necessary to his career ambitions. Negotiating priorities will get the boss's buy-in for his expanded duties. When the smoke clears, his accomplishments will be easier to see.

Flexible Maneuvering

Dear Readers,

Many people let rigidity get in the way of career plans, and they miss options. It's a stressful Striver characteristic to set up a plan and hold onto it like a pitbull clinging to the seat of your pants. The upside of this quality is perseverance. The downside is it will cause you to doggedly grasp your precious self-made plan even though it could be detrimental to your career. Many people are firmly holding onto ossified attitudes and meaningless goals when job duties change rapidly or slip out from under them and disappear. The best-laid Striver plans may be obsolete before the day is over. The point is to stay light on your feet and open to the unexpected.

In today's workplace, change is rapid and new skills are needed all the time. Constant reorganizations are very stressful for many people because previously valued skills are sometimes rendered useless. Instead of fixating on goals, it's critical to cast a wider net. Striver energy can be creative if you free it from constrictions. Many people develop careers out of sheer serendipity. To do this you have to be willing to let go of cherished plans when necessary.

Cartoonist Scott Adams, creator of the "Dilbert" comic strip, turned a hobby into a successful career when he got laid off. His cartoons reflect life in the workplace and his experiences. Getting laid off was his crisis, but with flexibility and ingenuity he turned it into a brand-new career. Crisis can be a growth experience and not a treadmill. It's all in how you look at it.

POSTSCRIPT

Is There Life After Work?

Dear Readers,

There are no more forty-hour workweeks. The rationalization for this has to do with the so-called realities of the world marketplace. If competitors are willing to work harder for less, then everyone must meet this challenge. This is a Striver stressful perception, because constant pressure to do more with less is unending. This stressful perception has to be questioned, because everyone, including yourself, expects that you must give

150 percent. When all about you are caught up in the heady excitement of making it big, how do you go home at a reasonable hour? It feels like the risk you'd be taking is enormous. You can kiss your career good-bye. To think about setting limits on Striver can feel like jumping off the cliff into an abyss.

To really change Striver you have to come to terms with the question, How do I get ahead without my Striver always in charge? When people decide to take on their Strivers and cut back their workweek, it usually means from fourteen hours a day to twelve. Further, they firmly vow to come in only every other weekend. But in doing so, they feel like shirkers.

CEOs who work eighty-hour weeks attempt to fire up their employees and give themselves a little shot of virtue by announcing, "I don't ask anything of my people that I don't expect from myself." Considering that most CEOs in America earn about 190 times more than their average employee, what does that tell you? Are you willing to give as much as your CEO for a fraction of the wages? If you are, then realize you are going to be in for a lot of stress, frustration, and eventual disappointment. Only a tiny fraction of you are ever going to make it to the executive "sweets." So it's up to you to decide where you fit in all this and what your values are. Stress rises when you come into conflict with your own values. If you value a holistic, well-rounded life and you're not leading one, you have to make some choices. You can't work all the time and still have a life after work.

The Telltale Smoke Signal

Striver is the Stress Personality that will render you most vulnerable to burnout. We're often told by people who attend stress programs that they're chided by colleagues with questions like, "Stress class? What's the matter, can't you stand the heat?" Yet in every seminar and class we conduct someone either is on the verge of burnout and quitting or has burned out, quit, and returned to the fray. They've come to the realization that they've got to learn how to handle stress to have a satisfying work life. "I didn't pay attention to the signals until I realized that I was trailing black smoke," is a common observation. One of the most striking features of burnout is loss of motivation, though most don't recognize it as a symptom of burnout. The highly competitive nature of today's workplace can also be a factor in burning up your motor. This important characteristic of Striver, competitiveness, bears watching.

Go to the courts and watch professionals and businessmen play racquetball for recreation. You will see them competing fiercely, sweating, grunting, and cursing. At the Jewish Community Center in San Francisco, their racquetball court was referred to as Cardiac Courts because so many men had heart attacks while playing.

Competitiveness stimulates the fight or flight response. This is a powerful physiological reaction nature built into us to deal with life-threatening danger. The cardiovascular system doesn't distinguish between real danger and a racquetball game. A steady diet of unceasing competition gives your body the message that you are in constant danger. Because of the Striver need to be competitive at all times, you pump the powerful chemicals adrenaline and noradrenaline into your cardiovascular system all day long. Add the Striver "need to win at all costs" attitude, and you increase the stress on your heart. If you spend every day in a highly competitive work atmosphere and then turn to competitive sports for recreation, you'd better be very healthy. Otherwise, you're asking for trouble.

Love as a Many-Splendored Stress Reducer

The Striver love affair with work can squeeze out all other lovers. In one workshop, a woman told us that she informed her prospective groom, "Honey, we can get married as planned, but I won't be able to go on the honeymoon because I have too much work." Much to her surprise, he was flabbergasted and angry.

At first he thought she was kidding. But when he realized she was serious, he told her that since they already had tickets and reservations, he was going on the trip alone. The idea of her new bridegroom honeymooning by himself brought her to her senses. She realized maybe she ought to fire her Striver if she wanted to have a marriage. Alas, you can't fire Striver. It is in no way fainthearted. Achievement needs are normal, so it is unlikely that you'll ever lose your drive permanently. The core concept to remember in controlling this powerful force is *balance*. Striver is seductive. Most people believe all their success in life can be attributed to this drive. But it can also render you one-dimensional, so zeroed in on achievement that you fail to enjoy your successes. Then striving incessantly seems hardly worth the effort.

The fast track has many hurdles. In this chapter we have outlined some of them and suggested how to bring balance into a life dominated by your Striver. We've talked about how to harness ambition and look realistically at Striver perfectionism. The workaholic all-or-nothing attitude was examined. Finally, we took a look at goal fixation—how it causes stress and how it limits career options.

QUICK REFERENCE STRESS TIPS FOR *STRIVER*

Use these stress tips to help keep your Striver in check. Some are in the chapter and some are from others who have found these ideas useful.

- Pay attention to your health.
- Be flexible and adjust to variable demands.
- Relax and enjoy life.
- Do your best and let it go at that.
- Take pleasure in each day's accomplishments.
- Enjoy your family.
- Leave work at work.
- Reevaluate expectations of yourself and others.
- Set reasonable work hours and leave at a certain time each day.
- Know your limits and accept that you need not be perfect.

CHAPTER 4

Critical Judge

Attack of the Killer Critic

How to Recognize *Critical Judge*

Jan has been on her job only a few months. After her first evaluation, she's despondent. Her manager pointed out an error she's been making fairly consistently and showed her how to rectify it. "Other than that, you're doing just fine," the manager said reassuringly. As Jan returns to her cube, a co-worker, Robin, asks how the evaluation went. "Not so good; it seems I'm making a lot of mistakes. But I guess I'm expected to be perfect," she replies defensively. She hurries away from Robin and sits down at her desk to review the evaluation. She can't stop ruminating about the mistake. "How could I be so stupid as to make the same error over and over?" she asks herself out loud.

This is a new industry, with terminology and methods foreign to her, although she's had similar experience on her last job. Jan is resentful at having to spend all her time catching up on work not done before she came, instead of getting the proper training. "How could I be expected to know everything when I had to learn it all myself?"

Jan has convinced herself that her performance has to be superior or she's not doing a good job. This means no mistakes, and a "goof" makes her nervous, depressed, and uncertain. Frustration festers inside her when she's unable to perform the way she wants. Sometimes it seems that the more perfect she tries to be, the more mistakes she makes.

The stress is beginning to tell. Jan no longer feels capable of doing a good job. On really bad days she avoids people, cries, and feels sorry for herself. At other times she's excessively critical of "lazy" colleagues such as Robin, who wastes the company's time talking to her boyfriend on the telephone. It bothers her no end that she takes her work so seriously and others don't. "Maybe Robin had better mind her own business, instead of heckling me about my evaluation," she mutters. There is a heckler here all right, but it isn't Robin; it's Jan's Critical Judge.

THE *CRITICAL JUDGE* STRESS TEST

Read the questions below and place a check (✔) in the appropriate column to the right to indicate your response. Find out how your Critical Judge beliefs and behaviors increase your stress. Pay attention to the questions you checked "Usually" and "Frequently." These have to be reduced to "Occasionally" or "Seldom" in order to control Critical Judge.	NEVER	SELDOM	OCCASIONALLY	FREQUENTLY	USUALLY
Do I: 1. Become disheartened when my work is criticized? 2. Use negative criticism on myself? 3. Lose confidence when I make a mistake? 4. Criticize and blame myself when decisions don't work out? 5. Concentrate on my faults to make myself a better person? 6. Consider all criticism of myself valid? 7. Get disgusted and perceive co-workers as indifferent performers? 8. Believe I have to be perfect to do a good job? 9. Feel it's necessary to attach blame when things don't go right? 10. Think that without Critical Judge I won't be successful?					

How *Critical Judge* Causes Stress

When Critical Judge constantly berates you, it's hard to stay out of the dumps. One result is a sense of worthlessness. Feeling inadequate, you hesitate to risk new ventures that could build your self-esteem. Then you feel stuck in the same old rut and criticize yourself for not seeking new challenges. Another result of Critical Judge inner assaults is depression, and psychological depression lowers the immune response, rendering you more vulnerable to disease.

Critical Judge acts like a mirror that reflects flaws both inwardly and outwardly. It's easy to see the defects of everyone else, including your manager, subordinate, colleagues, competitors, ad nauseum. It's very stressful to see fault everywhere, and it could backfire. You can be sure when this Stress Personality is tired of going out after someone else it won't be long before it turns on you.

Advice to the Job Stressed

The next four job stress cases illustrate the grief Critical Judge puts people through as they try to cope with the unpredictable stresses of work life.

"Attack of the Killer Critic" deals with how to handle criticism from others, both warranted and unwarranted. Put on the spot and feeling like a bad schoolboy chastised by the principal, "Attacked" fears he is overreacting. He learns that it's desirable to scan criticism, accept what he wants, and ignore the rest.

A working mom falls into the trap of condemning herself for not being a supermom in "Woman Stumbles on Mommy Track." Self-esteem plummets because of uncertainty about her competence as a mother. Confidence and self-esteem are boosted when she concentrates on her positives.

In "100 Percent Jerk," a subordinate spends 100 percent of her time bristling over the boss's lackadaisical attitude. The aggravation and stress are diminished as she learns to mind her own business and ignore his.

Perceived insults upset a dedicated engineer in "Engineer Shreds Office Mate." When he sees his work tossed aside by a group of eager beavers, he learns that insults are in the mind of the beholder and so are the faults of his office mate.

Read the "Dear Mary and Rene" letters. The replies to these letters will show you how to stay out of Critical Judge's courtroom.

STRESSOR TOPIC

HOW TO ACCEPT CRITICISM

The first example focuses on a very stressful topic for Critical Judge: how to accept criticism. When you have so much internal censure an innocuous remark or seemingly trivial comment can provoke an overreaction. This Stress Personality assumes all complaints about you are valid and aimed at putting you down. The remarks are blown out of proportion because you're getting it from both barrels, externally and internally.

Attack of the Killer Critic

Dear Mary and Rene,

I can't tolerate off-the-wall criticism, particularly from people who don't know anything about my job. I work with an operations manager who doesn't understand how our organization functions. When I attempt to explain to him how we operate, he acts like he knows my job, but he doesn't. He puts me on the spot and seems to doubt what I'm saying. I hate to meet with him and feel like I've been called to the principal's office.

His snide, pointed comments upset me, and I bite my tongue to keep from talking back to him. He acts disappointed in me, as if he would be happier if I worked elsewhere. I end up feeling at fault, though afterwards, when I think about it, I can't figure out what I did wrong. Even though I didn't ask him for suggestions on how to do my job, he insists on giving me unsolicited lectures. In private, I pore over his assessments to determine whether they're valid or not. Although I know the criticism is unwarranted, there's a part of me that always believes it's true. After one of these critical attacks I feel angry, persecuted, and depressed. Do you think I'm overreacting?

Donning the Dunce Cap

Dear Attacked,

There is no question you're overreacting, particularly since the unsolicited feedback may not even be valid. Furthermore, the overreaction doesn't address the salient point, which is how to handle criticism. Critical Judge makes it difficult for you to deal with the "principal." This Stress Personality accepts everything said as proof that you're incompetent, then hammers you with, "See, I told you so; others see it, too." The faulty perception is that since the information is conclusive, you are a bad person.

Critical Judge uses criticism as punishment, and you believe others use it that way, too. The assumption is that people are punishing you when they give you a negative opinion. Here are some of the stressful perceptions that rile you up in this matter:

- If your judgment is questioned you must be wrong.
- Self-interrogation will uncover your "crime."
- You need to defend yourself when criticized.

Your image of the manager as school principal is inappropriate in this case. The "interrogator" is really your Critical Judge. No amount of cross-examination will identify offenses you didn't really commit.

The purpose of this internal grilling is to specify the supposed faults so that you'll never fall prey to them again. However, there is no evidence this works to correct mistakes. Usually it has the opposite effect. It's so unpleasant to wallow around in your shortcomings that it feels better to try to defend yourself and get the charges dismissed.

A new perception is that you don't have to defend yourself because you haven't done anything wrong. The following stress tips provide some methods for handling criticism without punishing yourself.

STRESS TIPS   PROTECT YOUR FLANK, ACKNOWLEDGE YOUR FAULTS

Apply negative assertion to criticism.

To disarm critics, acknowledge your shortcomings. Admit that "Yes, sometimes I do make mistakes," or "I can see how you might think my ideas won't work." The key is not to get defensive. This is negative assertion, and it takes the wind out of the critic's sails. Instead, agree in principle that you're not perfect, nor do you need to be. Use this technique on your own Critical Judge as well. Make it clear to this part of yourself that you do not expect to be perfect, nor do you want to be. As soon as you learn to unload criticism you'll no longer be vulnerable to attacks of the killer critics.

Question your Critical Judge's assumptions.

One stressful practice of Critical Judge is the tendency to negatively color or distort what is said by others. Questions or comments become "snide and pointed" references to your inferiority. You get the "feeling" someone does not approve of you. These assumptions reinforce the certainty of your inferiority and give this Stress Personality more power over you.

Always check out a supposed criticism with the other person before you accept it. This challenges Critical Judge projections. For example, you can say to your manager, "I get the feeling you're disappointed with my work. Do we have a problem?" If he says, "Oh no, of course not," accept that and drop the matter. If he says, "Yes, we do," you have a foundation for talking about your real differences and resolving them.

View criticism as neutral feedback.

If criticism is not helpful, ignore it. If it is, use it as feedback. Try this analogy: Suppose a friend invited you to examine the contents of his garage prior to a spring cleaning sale. The friend tells you to take anything you like. You might find some tools or an old lamp you want, but you're not obligated to take everything. Even though the person offering you criticism doesn't know anything about your job, there might be something useful in what they say. When you're criticized, thank the other person and let them know you'll take the feedback under consideration. Think about it. Check it out with those who know you. If it doesn't seem to fit, discard it.

Stress Tips Summary

As long as Attacked takes criticism into court and tries to defend against it, failure is assured. There's no way to win against Critical Judge because this Stress Personality has lifetime tenure. Don't make this Stress Personality the court of last resort. Any appeal to this judge to ascertain guilt or innocence will always bring a guilty verdict. The stress tips will help Attacked stay out of the court altogether. Once free to question Critical Judge's assumptions, there's no need to defend against them.

TOPIC SUMMARY

Get Out of the Courtroom

Dear Readers,

This Stress Personality's judgments are generalized and nonspecific, which makes them difficult to defend against. For example, when you hear, "You always screw up," there is no way to respond to that indictment. Sometimes it might be true, but so what? You have to know what specifically you did wrong and request suggestions as to how to improve or fix it. You'll notice that Critical Judge is not eager to move toward solutions. So you have to nudge this part of yourself in that direction.

Critical Judge is mainly interested in assigning blame, not finding solutions. In fact, these accusations hinder the search for answers. When the focus is on "who dunnit?" there's no emphasis on "whadda we do now?" Trapped in shame and blame, you're so busy defending your actions, how could you possibly come up with new and innovative ideas? When you find yourself in the blame game, tell Critical Judge, "I don't care *that* it happened; I want to know what to do next."

Self-criticism is often more difficult to handle than criticism from others. It's insidious, because we make it up and then believe it, and it becomes much harder to defend against.

In the following letter, a working mom gets down on herself because she can't be Superwoman.

STRESSOR TOPIC

THE STRESS OF TRYING TO BE SUPERMOM

Working women stress themselves out by attempting to be perfect mothers and maintain domestic standards worthy of a Good Housekeeping Seal of Approval while balancing career and family life. Many try futilely to emulate their mothers who didn't work outside the home. They complain about husbands who don't do their share in helping them live up to their phantom standard of domestic excellence. Along with themselves, husbands and children become the target of Critical Judge disappointment as the following Advice example demonstrates.

Woman Stumbles on Mommy Track

Dear Mary and Rene,

My stress comes from trying to find a happy medium in a two-career family with a sometimes combative three-year-old son and two dogs. Added to the mix are my graduate school studies. My husband works long hours, too, and we're both tired when we get home. I criticize him for not doing more household chores. There is so much that needs to be done: laundry, dusting, cleaning, mopping, and vacuuming. I get angry that he doesn't volunteer to help. He's either lazy or inconsiderate, and every time I have to ask him to help, it ends in an argument. I get depressed because I can't keep the house in perfect order. Then I criticize myself and feel upset, lousy, and mean. I often feel like I'm failing as a parent. On the weekends I'm either studying or cleaning house, and I feel guilty for not playing with my son. This makes me anxious, sad, and drained, and my self-esteem plummets. Because my husband and I are so busy, we tend to avoid dealing with all this tension. It seems impossible to live up to my high standards, but I can't stop criticizing myself for failing. How do I quit being so critical of myself and my husband?

Flunking Home Life

Dear Mommy Track,

You're being too hard on everyone, especially yourself. It appears that the only ones safe from your Critical Judge's scolding are the dogs. Beware: this Stress Personality specializes in unflattering labels and will cause you to see yourself and your loved ones in a distorted way. To your Critical Judge, your husband is lazy, your son is suffering from a lack of attention, and you are failing as a parent. No wonder you feel discouraged. To better understand how this Stress Personality affects you, read over the following Critical Judge stressful perceptions:

- You are a failure as a parent.
- You're too busy to deal with the tension.
- If your husband doesn't share your standards, he's lazy.

Finding fault and placing blame are Critical Judge's way of trying to "improve" you and your family. But these traits make the stress worse because there is no defense against them. When you try to keep the house in perfect order it's a setup for Critical Judge. Since it's impossible, Critical Judge always has something to condemn you for. A new perception is "This is not a time in my life when I can have a perfect house, and that's OK." It really is impossible to live up to your high standards, and it's time to give them up.

You have to deal with tension between you and your husband no matter how busy you are. Otherwise, the tension feeds your Critical Judge and provides this Stress Personality with another example of how you're flunking home life. A new perception is that you're lucky your husband doesn't have the same standards you do, or he would add to the Critical Judge chorus of condemnation.

To help you pass the home life test, consider the following stress tips.

STRESS TIPS   CUT YOURSELF SOME SLACK

Use "thought stopping."

A good technique for tuning out Critical Judge is *thought stopping*. Identify and accept Critical Judge as a part of yourself. This gives the process of negative self-criticism a "persona" you can talk to as a separate entity. When you hear the negative criticism, firmly say "Stop" or "No" until the Critical Judge attack passes. Then demand that Critical Judge give you two positive statements about yourself, your husband, or your son. If necessary, write the positive feedback down. This will retrain Critical Judge. Tell your husband what you are doing and enlist his help.

Change your standards.

Lower your standards to B or even B minus. In your current circumstances you will not be able to maintain a perfect household grade point average. Resist the Critical Judge attempts to motivate you with condemnatory remarks so that you will try harder. How much harder can you try? Your standards are unrealistic. You can't win a debate with this Stress Personality. If you focus on the house, you will be slammed for not spending more time with your son. If you do the latter, you're a lousy housekeeper. Decide where it's most important to concentrate your attention: your child or the housework. Talk it over with your husband and figure out together what's most important.

Re-capture your self-worth by assuming you are a good parent.

A new perception is that you are leading a most impressive life, successful at your job while in graduate school and married with a family. It's amazing that you or your husband have any time left over to clean your house at all. When you look back at your life someday, think about what you'd like to grade yourself on. That you kept a perfect house under difficult circumstances? Or that you were a loving, attentive mom who got to spend enriching time with her son before he grew up? One senior mom told us, "I'm sorry that when my kids wanted me to take them to the park, I often said no because I felt I had to keep the house spic and span. Looking back, the pleasure of being with my kids far outweighed any pleasure in keeping a 'perfect house.'

Stress Tips Summary

These stress tips will help Mommy Track gain a fresh perspective on her life. Her negative judgments about herself and her husband will diminish when she gives herself credit for doing as well as she is.

TOPIC  SUMMARY

Keeping Your Balance on the Mommy Track

Dear Readers,

There is continuing domestic warfare over housework in the families of working couples. It's one thing to hassle with your kids over domestic chores, because you have authority. But it's not so easy to do the same with a husband, whether you try ordering him, shaming him, or appealing to his sense of fair play. Many husbands approach the subject from an Inner Con Artist point of view.

One female attorney told us that her husband, a high school principal, couldn't figure out how to separate the colored laundry from the white and therefore couldn't perform the complicated task of washing clothes. Her Critical Judge skewered him with sarcasm, pejorative comments about his intelligence, and other criticisms designed to humiliate him into doing his share, but to no avail. It wasn't until she recognized his Inner Con Artist that she realized she had to be more direct and not jab him with Critical Judge barbs. They figured out how to trade and share chores. Obviously he didn't like laundry detail, so she took it on in return for his cleaning the refrigerator, a chore she detested.

When we sent this squabble out over our e-mail newsletter, we received some creative suggestions on how to resolve this fight. One woman's compromise was that she would do the housework half the time, and if her mate didn't want to do the other half, he had to hire a cleaning person and pay for it. He did and it worked out fine. This compromise succeeded because they stopped hassling and figured out an acceptable solution.

Another bone of contention for supermoms is not being satisfied with *how* hubby does his share. His efforts are met with dissatisfaction because he doesn't clean to her standards. So he cleans up the kitchen. Then she comes in like an army inspector general and declares, "This is unacceptable." He says, "To whom?" and they're into it again. The solution is that when it's her night to clean the kitchen, she does it the way she wants. When it's his night, she accepts his efforts and stays out of the kitchen. It's a no-fault solution that will keep Critical Judge out of the house.

When Critical Judge starts zeroing in on people whose behavior you find offensive, it causes aggravation and stress. When it's your husband and family it's one thing, but when it's your boss, the irritation and contempt can create serious troubles on your job.

STRESSOR TOPIC

HOW TO STOP HATING YOUR BOSS

Bad bosses get a lot of ink these days. Books and articles have been written about them. There's even an annual contest to find the worst boss in America. We have no shortage of such descriptions in our research. One boss punished a subordinate for getting married at an inconvenient time and for going on her honeymoon. Her hours were doubled the week before the wedding, and when she returned, her boss labeled her as having an "attitude problem." A working mom reported that when she requested time to get her ill child from daycare and take her home, she was refused. The boss suggested she could bring the child back to the office and let the kid rest on the floor. Another boss got hysterical and began screaming at a subordinate who questioned a directive.

Bosses have been accused of being not only incompetent but perhaps even insane. They're described as overbearing, disorganized, mean, patronizing, power mad, and nit-picking control freaks. Boss hating belongs to several different Stress Personalities, but we will be looking at it here from the Critical Judge point of view. The following Advice example shows how a woman gets overly stressed by labeling and disliking her boss.

The 100 Percent Jerk

Dear Mary and Rene,

I have a supervisor who doesn't take an interest in the work he assigns. He won't give me the help or resources to do the job. In our staff meetings he lectures us like he's addressing congress. Most of what he says is irrelevant and of no practical use. He's forgetful, and he's always busy doing paperwork or going to the racquetball club during work hours and getting paid for it. Every morning and after lunch for about one hour he and his cronies (all men) sit around and shoot the bull about fishing, sports, the weekend, etcetera.

Sometimes a couple of other supervisors join them; again, they're both men. (As you've obviously guessed, I'm a woman.) They seem oblivious to the fact that other people are working, trying to meet deadlines and scurrying around. They just sit there and BS. I've told his manager what's going on, but he doesn't seem to care. I get upset, angry, and short tempered. In an effort to relax when I tense up, I practice deep breathing to the point where it makes me light headed. I toss things around on my desk just to disturb them. The boss doesn't even notice. It usually takes me an hour to calm down after he finally goes to work.

He's truly a person too nervous to steal and too lazy to work. He's 75 percent Con Artist, 25 percent Pleaser, and a 100 percent jerk. Why should I do a decent job on something if he isn't even going to look at it? I do it because of pride in my work, but I'm so disgusted by what he gets away with that I feel like quitting. How do I keep him from getting my goat?

Lazy Boss Gets Subordinate's Goat

Dear Disgusted,

Your stress is being caused as much by your Critical Judge as by this supervisor. The number of accusations you're making is a tip-off. You say he's lazy, forgetful, a time stealer, and a prize jerk. It's not what he's doing that causing you stress, it's what you're doing to yourself. Every time he does something you dislike, it sets off a stress response in you. Even hyperventilating doesn't seem to help. The trouble with fixating so much on his misdeeds is that you set the Critical Judge trial procedure in motion. Your Critical Judge could even decide you're a jerk for doing the work while he's off playing. Instead of putting him on the pillory, focus on the most important issue you bring up: You can't get the resources you need from him. The ability to do your job is in jeopardy. Turn your attention to that, because it's far more important than whether or not he gets away with misbehaving. Pay attention to the reactions that lead you in the wrong direction. You

- Let the work habits of others cause you stress
- Judge the performance of your boss by your standards
- Feel bad over something you can't do anything about

These actions will keep you mired in the muck of this unpleasant environment. People report to us that it's exhausting to be trapped in this daily activity of catching others doing something wrong. You'll get a lot of your energy back when you consider that if this boss is so outrageous it will not go unnoticed forever. Others can take some responsibility for correcting him. If your complaints continually fall on deaf ears, you can assume you're being heard as a "complainer." When people turn off and ignore you, it's a clue that Critical Judge has taken on the task of exposing managerial wrongdoing.

Disengage from the agitation.

It sounds like you're agitated a good part of the day. You get worked up while he's gone to the racquetball club. You get worked up every morning for an hour and every afternoon for an hour when he's gabbing with his cronies. And after he's back at his desk, it takes you another hour to cool off and stop hyperventilating. This is too much stress to waste on a 100 percent jerk. The more you concentrate on feeling pride in your work instead of agitation, the better you'll feel. Concentrated attention on your duties will help you disengage. When you are fully focused, Critical Judge will be locked out of the office.

Focus on getting gratification from the work you do.

You mentioned working for self-pride. Bravo. That's the attitude to balance the negativity of your Critical Judge. Practice the fine art of concentrating on your own duties, and tune him out. You're letting him control your work environment. By no means cover up for him. Just do your own job and let the chips fall where they may. When the boss's goofing off becomes a concern to his boss, the chips may fall in your lap. Keep reminding yourself you work for the company not the supervisor.

Go after the resources you need to do your job.

If you've labeled this manager correctly as a 75 percent Con Artist, you've got to change strategies to get the resources you need. He won't like unpleasant encounters, and if he picks up your Critical Judge undertone, he'll avoid you like the plague. You could offer to locate the resources yourself and tell him exactly how you intend to accomplish this. He'll feel relieved that he doesn't have to do it. He can play an extra game of racquetball, and you can get ahead on your job. It's a prospective win-win. The end cycle of Inner Con Artist behavior is to push the limits until self-destruction is assured. So you, with your diligence at ferreting out resources and meeting deadlines, will be noticed and rewarded.

Stress Tips Summary

When Disgusted lets go of her Critical Judge indignation at the boss, she will reduce her stress and increase her efficiency, something she can be proud of. It's demoralizing when you think you're voicing legitimate complaints but others are turning you off because they don't want to listen. You believe you're the herald of right-teousness and they think you're a pain in the ass. Critical Judge will put you in that position.

TOPIC SUMMARY

The Stress of Fault Finding

Dear Reader,

The faults of this supervisor seem minor compared to some of the ones we described in the introduction to this section. If the worst traits Disgusted ever encounters in a boss are that he BS's with cronies and sneaks out to play racquetball, she'll be lucky. It's hard to like people and enjoy your job when you are looking for flaws. There is no shortage of human defects that can be uncovered if you're looking for them.

Fault finding can easily escalate. In this case the spotlight went from the male boss to the entire male gender. There definitely is antagonism between the sexes, though in today's diversity-conscious workplace, attempts are being made to create better understanding. Men stand around shooting the bull and women gather to gossip. Both of these are negative stereotypes and damning evidence for Critical Judge generalizations. We've found that Stress Personalities are not gender specific, and stereotypes rarely apply. The hard-nosed boss who banned the subordinate's honeymoon was a woman; the hysterical screamer was a man.

Whoever your boss is, you can count on having another one before you know it. This is the Mary Dempcy "roulette wheel of management" theory. The quality of your work life depends on where you land, just as the outcome of roulette depends on which color you land on, red or black. You land on red and acquire a manager you can't get along with. Try as you might, you can't figure out why this one doesn't like you. You've always gotten glowing reports about your work from managers, and as far as you can tell, your quality is the same as always. So what's different? This time you landed on red. But never fear; before too long you'll be reorganized and you'll land on black, acquiring a manager who's perfect for you. All it takes is to stay in the game.

Criticism directed toward others sometimes results from misinterpreting intentions. Bad feelings and wounded pride will trigger a Critical Judge reaction. In the next Advice example, an engineer's Critical Judge flails out in all directions in response to what he considers an insult to his professional skill.

STRESSOR TOPIC

HOW TO TAKE THE INJURY OUT OF INSULT

Critical Judge is particularly vulnerable to perceived insults. That's because this part of yourself is constantly on the lookout for evidence of your unworthiness. But insults are subject to interpretation. We call people who are virtually immune to insults "thickskinned." Or we might call them "brain-dead"— so out of it, they don't know when they're being put down. But there are advantages to blowing off potential insults. For one thing, you deprive Critical Judge of ammo to drill you with. If you don't take what's said as an insult, there are no hurtful words for Critical Judge to feel piqued about. In the following case, a thin-skinned engineer loses face when he perceives his hard work is tossed aside.

Engineer Shreds Office Mates

Dear Mary and Rene,

Several efforts have been made to create a common test procedure for use by all test engineers in my group. The idea is to standardize our function. I was assigned the job of creating this procedure nine months ago and felt pride in the work I had done. The group that was supposed to do the next phase of my procedure junked my efforts and started all over with a new design. Now a third group led by a contractor is attempting to do one. A fourth group is officially assigned to create the standardization, but their test engineer doesn't want to. So they are just ignoring it.

I am frustrated, insulted, and mad because they threw out all my work. It upsets me to see this project screwed up. I've attempted to convince my manager to stop group three and make group four do the job they were assigned. I criticize the contractor from group three and the staff engineer from group four in discussions with my manager. Lately, out of exasperation, I've been criticizing my office mate, who was part of group two. I'd like to quit shredding my co-worker and everyone else. How do I stop focusing on everything I dislike about this mess?

Shredding the Wrong Evidence

Dear Shredder,

Your Critical Judge has spared no one in this matter. Notice that you've singled out one person from each group to heap your scorn on. Negative criticism is an ineffective expression of anger. Potshots sometimes hit the mark, but they do nothing to reduce your stress. Your Critical Judge is lashing out in all directions. The more stress you're under, the more Critical Judge finger pointing you do. It sounds like you got hooked by your Striver when you started the job. You refer to "my [test] procedure." Striver took complete ownership, and even though the project was handed off, Striver thinks it still belongs to you. When it got junked, you fell into Critical Judge because your pride was hurt and you felt insulted. Here are some of the stressful perceptions clouding your vision:

- Criticizing others will make you feel better.
- It's an insult when your efforts are discarded.
- If your work is ignored it means it's no good.

At the crux of all your stress and critical judgment is the belief that the other groups have rejected you by not accepting your work. This is taken as a personal insult. Critical Judge cannot resist telling you that you are a failure because they didn't respect what you did.

It's likely that the quality of your work had nothing to do with the fact that it was ignored. You are dealing with Striver behavior in the other people. In typical Striver fashion, group two had to ignore your work and start all over to build a better mousetrap. A bunch of Strivers won't consider the project a success unless they think up all the ideas themselves. Because it's painful to be on the receiving end of Critical Judge's stern sentences, you're shifting all the inner negative feelings about your alleged failure onto others. But carping, shredding, complaining, and trying to get your manager after their hides isn't going to make you feel any better. You have to reinterpret events without Critical Judge input. First, examine the intent of the group who "junked" your procedure.

STRESS TIPS FOCUSING ON THE REAL ISSUE

Reinterpret the intent of others.

 Ask yourself if your interpretation of an event hurts your feelings. If so, get a different perspective. Look at how you punished yourself. The Strivers "junked" your work, which is taken as an insulting implication that your work is junk. But who labeled it that way? Guess who. No wonder you're upset.

You can be sure a group of Strivers didn't even bother to look at your work, because it wasn't theirs. It's in the nature of Strivers to consider their own ideas as best. A new perception is that a group full of Strivers couldn't have done anything else but reinvent the wheel. The new take on their intentions is that what they did had absolutely nothing to do with you or your efforts. Look for an intent that doesn't make you feel miserable, and Critical Judge will be tempered.

Let go of stressful entanglements you don't need.

 From what you're saying, it sounds like you handed this project off to group two and it's no longer yours—especially since they ignored your work and started over. Let them have the headache if they've taken it on. It sounds like this whole venture is a hot potato. Why do you want to get burned? You now have no ownership of this project. If it turns into a mess, your pride won't suffer. You can even say, "I told you so." It's your manager's responsibility to drive this task, so let him. Accept the fact that you did a good job and feel positive about it.

Accentuate the positive.

 It's good that you'd like to figure out how to stop ragging on your office mate. It shows that you want to control Critical Judge. Give your co-worker the benefit of the doubt and focus on the things you like about him. Compliment him once in a while. When differences arise between you, discuss them calmly and objectively. Forget about the lost time on this project, and treat all three other efforts more objectively. Whenever you hear a negative comment, identify three positive ways to look at things. If you do this consistently you will retrain this part of your-self. It will lower your stress and retire this Judge to his chambers. Remember: The best way to stop criticizing others is to stop doing it to yourself.

Stress Tips Summary

Shredder needs to step back and reevaluate his role in this drama of chaos. Because he never let go of the project he started, its failure to progress is translated into a personal failure of his. These conditions are ripe for an internal assault on his competency by Critical Judge. Adding to his stress is a sense that if he could somehow control all these other colleagues he could insure success. The stress tips will provide him with a more objective perspective. He'll realize that the project's status doesn't constitute a failure on his part.

TOPIC SUMMARY

Take Off the Hair Shirt

Dear Readers,

If you recognize that you're being stung by insults, suspect that Critical Judge is in there stirring up the hornets' nest. This part of you thinks a jab at your wounded ego will galvanize you into renewed effort to prove to the world that you're OK. All this anguish can be short-circuited by giving both yourself and the other person the benefit of the doubt. Assume that their motives are benign and there is no reason to put you down, because you're OK. To paraphrase Eric Berne, "I'm OK, you're OK," and the hair shirt can come off.

There is a difference between an insult and a perceived insult. Critical Judge scans the world for prospective aspersions. Derogatory comments, whether real or imagined, are a form of rejection, and inoffensive remarks are interpreted as affronts. Critical Judge injects unflattering meaning, which leads to wounded pride. Survival instincts are stirred up. People get angry and energized to do something about rejection, especially when it strikes to the heart of one's professional capabilities. The first reaction is to defend, then strike back at the alleged offender by denigrating their competency. Then you compare yourself to the other person in order to come out looking better. This seems to provide some relief from Critical Judge, but it's a stressful and useless maneuver. In reality, you're really defending yourself against Critical Judge, who conjured up the insult in the first place. Examine what was said carefully and decide whether you want to give it all the negative energy it takes to consider it an insult. If not, there's no injury and no insult.

POSTSCRIPT

Here Comes the Judge

Dear Readers,

In many industries, especially the high-tech field, it's common for new technologies to be invented all the time. There are no precedents, but there are always time constraints. You not only have to create a new product but must do so in a hurry before some competitor beats you to the punch. You need a great deal of self-confidence to tackle such a challenge. Faced with this predicament, Critical Judge causes you to denigrate yourself for not automatically knowing how to do what's never been done. This is cruel and unusual self-punishment. Self-esteem takes a hit, because in Critical Judge's tortuous reasoning, too much self-esteem will give you a swelled head. Unfortunately, the opposite of a swelled head is a deflated ego. Now you question your competency. Without a sense of competence you lose self-esteem and confidence in your abilities.

One buyer in a workshop told us that he had to develop purchasing guidelines for a brand-new product that incorporated a newly invented technology. He was constantly under fire from a group of managers about why he priced a particular item the way he did. Under pressure from their Critical Judge scrutiny, along with his own, he was running himself ragged trying to justify his pricing decisions. Nothing satisfied them.

Finally, we helped him realize that he had been doing this work much longer than any of those pressuring him, and he was the expert. In fact, most of them knew nothing about pricing. They were expressing uneasiness due to their ignorance. He went back to work and began reassuring them, not with mounds of figures to justify his choice but by simply labeling himself "the expert." To his surprise, nobody questioned his new title, and all were greatly relieved. You have to block Critical Judge from downplaying your abilities. Critical Judge will hold you back by telling you, "You can't try that; you don't know how to do it." A new perception to counter this is, "I will know after I try it. I usually succeed."

Perfectionism Revisited

So you've decided to strike off on a course no one has ever taken. Just as you're about to take the first step, Critical Judge bars the way with the admonition, "If you're going to do this, it had better be perfect." This stops you cold because you fear the impact of Critical Judge disdain when you make the unavoidable mistakes. Critical Judge is your Monday morning quarterback critiquing miscues after the fact: "Why didn't you think of that before?" "How could you have made a blunder like this?" The only way to never make a mistake is to be perfect.

Perfectionism is a stressor for Critical Judge, as it is for Striver. The difference is that Striver seeks perfection to enhance self-image and obtain a sense of superiority. In the case of Critical Judge, perfection is sought to avoid this Stress Personality's inevitable wrath and scorn when you're not perfect. The outcome of not allowing yourself latitude to make mistakes or bad decisions is that you become too cautious. There is an appropriate cliché which addresses this point: If you never make a mistake or fail, you're not risking enough. Make it clear to Critical Judge that it's fine to take chances, whether you win or lose. This is how you grow and become immune to the negative effects of occasional failure. A new perception is: Perfectionism gets in the way of personal growth.

Building You Up by Running You Down

The Critical Judge demand for perfection is a misguided effort to motivate you. According to this Stress Personality, you are best motivated by concentrating on your faults. Dedicated to this view, compliments are filtered out and discarded. Critical Judge sneers, "Obviously they don't really know you, or they wouldn't have paid you a compliment." A comical version of this is Groucho Marx's famous quote, "I'd never join a club that would have me as a member."

People with severe Critical Judges hunger for positive strokes yet often brush them off or don't recognize them. This was particularly well illustrated in one of our programs. A woman complained that her boss was very critical and never praised her. But in fact, she had a litany of complaints about him that clearly came from her own Critical Judge. One was that he had insulted her. But after she recognized that it was her Critical Judge who interpreted the event, she reinterpreted it from a whole new perspective: "One day on his to way lunch, my manager stopped by my desk. Tucked under his arm was a copy of *One-Minute Manager.* He proceeded to give me a one-minute praising. It was so obvious what he was doing that I was embarrassed for both of us. After he walked away with a smugly satisfied expression on his face, I said to myself, 'That SOB. Who does he think he is to use a technique out of a book on me? He must think I'm too dumb to catch on.' But now I'm seeing this in a different light. There was nothing wrong with what he did; it was my Critical Judge who was interpreting his action and wouldn't let me accept his praise."

Although this part of you can come across as a real downer, remember that the behavior pattern has vestigial survival value. There is an unconscious purpose to the criticism. As with your fourth grade teacher who used to scold you for your own good, the motive is character improvement. But Critical Judge doesn't let up until you stop listening. You will be motivated to do your best when you challenge Critical Judge's motivational efforts. For real motivation, you need to take the sting out of the killer critic's reviews.

QUICK-REFERENCE STRESS TIPS FOR *CRITICAL JUDGE*

The following quick-reference tips come from people we've trained. When you get trapped in the courtroom with Critical Judge, use them to argue your case.

- Suffer the fools; without them the rest of us wouldn't look so good.
- One mistake doesn't make you a failure.
- Tell yourself that though you're not perfect, you're perfectly good.
- Focus on the positive.
- Ask for positive comments about your work.
- Accept the fact that you don't have to know everything to do a good job.
- Take what is useful from criticism; disregard the rest.
- Look for the good qualities in others and yourself.
- Concentrate on your own work instead of criticizing the performance of less motivated colleagues.
- Judge the performance, not the performer.

CHAPTER 5

Internal Timekeeper

Too Much to Do, Too Little Time

How to Recognize *Internal Timekeeper*

Greg rushes through the office door, throws a quick hello to the new receptionist, and dashes down the hall to a meeting of the customer support group. Greg is twenty minutes late. He recently moved and is still underestimating the amount of additional time it now takes to get to work. Hit with the sudden realization that he doesn't know which room the meeting is in, he hastily spins around to run back and find out from the receptionist, and he bumps into a colleague. "The meeting is tomorrow, not today," the co-worker says, smiling at Greg, who displays a mixture of dismay and relief. He would have known this was the wrong day if he'd looked at his Daytimer. Unfortunately, in his hurry to get out the door, he'd left it home, but then it's so chock-full of lists and scribbles between the lines and margins that he can't read it anyway.

In addition to all his other responsibilities, Greg has a deadline for his current project. He can't concentrate on it because he's bombarded all day with a constant stream of e-mail messages and phone calls. This disrupts his already scattered attention. Anxiety wells up in him as he mentally lists all the other things still to do. With a groan he remembers he can't work all weekend as planned because he promised his wife to landscape the front yard. He's been putting her off for months, and she is adamant that it must be done.

Skipping lunch as usual, Greg buckles down to try to prioritize his work for the rest of the day. But everything seems to be a priority and has to be done before he goes home. Just as he ploughs into his mountain of work, a buddy calls with the news that a notice is pinned to the downstairs bulletin board announcing that Greg's car lights have been left on. "Omigod," he mutters. "I do not have time to deal with Triple A."

Exhausted by the end of the day, he drives home with a splitting headache. When he walks through the door, his boys jump him with exuberant greetings. "Get these kids out of here," he yells at his wife. Things seem out of control. Greg's Internal Timekeeper is speeding him through life.

How *Internal Timekeeper* Causes Stress

Time-pressured anxiety is the scourge of today's working person and the basic emotional state of Internal Timekeeper. When in the vortex of this whirlwind you'll feel tense, jumpy, rushed, confused, and unable to sit still. Now matter how much you do, you're pressured by all the work piling up and you fret about what you can't get to. Add time pressure and you have the driving force of Internal Timekeeper stress. As work pressures increase, so does internal agitation, which triggers the need to do more and leaves you feeling overextended and exhausted. There is no rest, however, because there's always more to do. Internal Timekeeper is like a strict parent who insists you can't leave the table until you clean up your plate. The assembly line of tasks never stops. This endless pressure toward activity is the nexus that links you to Internal Timekeeper stress.

Advice to the Job Stressed

Job stress caused by Internal Timekeeper hyper-busyness and what to do about it is the subject of the next Advice examples. "Overextended Analyst Stretches Time" debunks the notion that you can create more time. Although the day gets stretched, work is never finished as more finds its way into the schedule, and the "To Do" list grows until it's out of hand.

In "Multitasker Caught in Crossfire," the Internal Timekeeper penchant for trying to juggle many things at once gets activated by the need to multitask several high-priority assignments. Once set in motion, however, the scattered, disorganized quality of this Stress Personality can't be controlled until concentration is focused.

"Invasion of the Intruders" illustrates close encounters of an unwanted kind: interruptions from frantic co-workers and a demanding boss who upset the workday of a person trying to plan a schedule. His interrupt-driven circus can be controlled when applying the Internal Timekeeper stress tips.

THE *INTERNAL TIMEKEEPER* STRESS TEST

Read the questions below and place a check (✔) in the appropriate column to the right to indicate your response. Find out how your Internal Timekeeper beliefs and behaviors increase your stress. Pay attention to the questions you checked "Usually" and "Frequently." These have to be reduced to "Occasionally" or "Seldom" in order to control Internal Timekeeper.	NEVER	SELDOM	OCCASIONALLY	FREQUENTLY	USUALLY
Do I: 1. Often feel rushed or hurried when working? 2. Feel irritated, confused, or scattered when interrupted? 3. Take on more work than I can handle in a given amount of time? 4. Seem to always be in a hurry to make up for lost time? 5. Become disorganized and less efficient under pressure? 6. Find myself preoccupied with one task while performing another? 7. Become terse, abrupt, or short with people when I'm interrupted? 8. Feel I'm falling further behind no matter how much time I spend at work? 9. Tend to switch tasks too often and have trouble concentrating on any one thing? 10. Make a "To Do" list each day that I never finish?					

In the last Advice example, "Man Works Like Dog," a frazzled production supervisor driven by Internal Timekeeper can find no way to manage a work and home life. The advice is aimed at how to "get a life" which means limiting work when it intrudes on home time.

This chapter discusses how Internal Timekeeper pushes people to the edge, monopolizes their time, and creates a frenzied life of endless activity. You will learn how to slow down this most prevalent of Stress Personalities.

Read the "Dear Mary and Rene" letters. The replies to these letters will help you bring Internal Timekeeper under control.

STRESSOR TOPIC

HOW TO KEEP YOURSELF FROM STRETCHING YOURSELF TOO THIN

This example illustrates the stress of doing too much. People attempt to handle work overload by trying to stretch time. A favorite Internal Timekeeper tool is the ubiquitous "To Do" list. First the list is created to help flag the blizzard of items one must tackle at the beginning of each day. Then you become enslaved by it. This list, which starts as a servant, becomes a tyrant. Internal Timekeeper is the overseer who cracks the whip and dictates how your time will be spent. Because the list is so long, you try to create more time by expanding the day. In the following example, a financial analyst pushes the time barrier and learns to speed up by slowing down.

Overextended Analyst Stretches Time

Dear Mary and Rene,

Help! I need more time. My workload on any given day is enough to keep me busy for a week. During a recent reorg I was assigned new duties. Because of cutbacks there is no requisition for another hire. I'm doing two jobs at once with no relief in sight. There isn't time to take care of the responsibilities I've already been assigned, let alone new ones. I'm trying to get caught up by coming in earlier, working longer hours, and taking work home with me. I gave up taking lunch long ago and now eat at my desk, courtesy of Chef Vending Machine. Still, there aren't enough hours in the day. In order to improve my efficiency and make sure nothing falls through the cracks, I create a daily "To Do" list. But it seems to increase the stress because I can never get to all the items. The unfinished tasks on the list are always on my mind and increase the pressure. I'm constantly frazzled, confused, and short of time. I'm frustrated because no matter how hard I try, I can't catch up. How do I make time for everything?

Stretching Time—The Cosmic Joke

Dear Timeless,

You can't make time for everything, because your Internal Timekeeper has taken on too much. The first choice of this Stress Personality when confronted with time limits is to try to expand or stretch time like a cosmic rubber band. Internal Timekeeper usually suggests you get up earlier, stay later, and work evenings and weekends. Although these seem like logical ways to relieve the pressure, they're ineffective because the more time you make available, the more the work expands to fill it. This is an example of Parkinson's Law. If you engage in this behavior you will have less time but more work than ever, and your ultimate reward is exhaustion.

To get a firm hold on this part of yourself you have to come to grips with these Internal Timekeeper stressful perceptions. If you

- Work long enough hours, you'll get caught up
- Make "To Do" lists you'll get to everything
- Skip lunch and breaks you'll make or save time

There's no way to makeup for lost time, because it can't be "lost" or "gained." That's a new perception. There are only so many hours in every day, and some are needed for work, some for home life, and some for rest. The Internal Timekeeper method of making up for lost time is to steal it from non-work-related activities. You can get up at the crack of dawn and burn the midnight oil, but you still have not increased the number of hours in the day.

Working longer hours to get caught up won't help either. Parkinson's Law is also Internal Timekeeper's law. Every task has three or four more components to which you could devote yourself. Since Internal Timekeeper's job is to think up things to keep you busy, the possibilities are endless. You can't stretch time, so you have to shrink the amount of work. The following stress tips will show you how.

STRESS TIPS   DON'T STRETCH TIME—SHRINK TASKS

Reduce the items on your "To Do" list.

Assume you are doing too much and need to pare down your precious "To Do" list. Prioritize the items by giving each a number. Limit yourself to a one, two, or three ranking. Next, select only the number one items, and make a new list with number one items only. This becomes your new "To Do" list. Put the other one away and out of sight. You can revisit the secondary list and go through the same steps after you've completed number one. As you are confronted with new items, place them on a "New Item" list and prioritize those the same way. To counter Internal Time-keeper's nervous concern about the subjects you shelved, assure yourself that if they are important they will surface again as a priority. Remem-ber, this Stress Personality will try to convince you that every item is a number one. Don't let this part of yourself make the final determination.

Allot a specific amount of time to a task.

After you've decided on a reasonable amount of time to complete a job, concentrate on it until you've used up the allot-ment and then stop. Go on to the next task, or if your workday is finished, leave. This same tech-nique works well at home. Instead of doing housework and chores until you drop, decide on how long you want to clean or do laundry, set a time when you'll stop, then go sit down and relax.

Before you start, tell your Internal Timekeeper, "It's 1 P.M. now. I will clean the house until 3 P.M., then I will knock off and be satisfied with what I've done." Home chores, like work tasks, are end-less. There's never a finish, and you can become a slave to both.

Stress Tips Summary

When Timeless follows these tips, she will discover that much of the work could be better organized, thereby reducing the time it takes. All the tips will help her apply self-discipline. Her "To Do" list will be priori-tized. As she works within allot-ted time frames, she'll be more efficient and won't waste time. These steps will also calm her down and she'll get more done.

TOPIC   SUMMARY

The Time of Your Life

Dear Readers,

Internal Timekeeper is a firm believer in the notion that if you work longer hours you will be more productive. Yet there is no evidence this makes people more efficient. In our research, many people report that their effec-tiveness diminishes with longer hours. When work hours are cut, produc-tivity goes up. However, the trick is to convince Internal Timekeeper of this. Long hours are a futile attempt to stretch time.

There has been a change in the way people look at time and work. Not so many years ago you worked a predictable schedule, 9 to 5, or 8:30 to 4:30, and you fit the amount of work you had to do into the time slot avail-able. Today, however, work has changed. Now people work on "projects," all of which have deadlines that are rarely met, but that nevertheless cause pressure. Now you have to finish the work no matter how long it takes. Downsizing means you take on more projects and nowadays work is much like piecework. You are expected to labor until you finish your "piece."

Time-limited deadlines and fast turnaround times increase time-pressured anxiety, the core of Internal Timekeeper. When you have too much to do and not enough time, you can't reduce the amount of work, so you try to increase time itself. You fool yourself into thinking there are more hours in the day than there are, so you increase the amount of work you become available for. You can't create more time, but you can create more pressure and stress on yourself. Eventually you wear down, and your work effectiveness inevitably diminishes.

People in their fifties naturally downsize their lifetime "To Do" lists because at that age they know time is limited. Then they begin to prioritize and decide what's really important to them. Some of the things they'd always thought they would do someday have to be given up. But it isn't felt as a loss. Rather it feels like a gift of time to finally devote themselves to things that really matter to them. Life passes very swiftly.

If your day is already stretched to the limit, how do you get more done? Many beleaguered people make the Internal Timekeeper choice to do several things at once. This gives rise to a hydra-headed monster of diffuse activity called *multitasking,* discussed in the next column.

STRESSOR TOPIC

HANDLING THE STRESS OF MULTITASKING

When companies require employees to wear several hats, juggling more than one job is routine. Force reduction (layoffs) means people have to learn to manage two or three totally different jobs at once. Another sanitized Orwellian term has been coined to describe this phenomenon: *multitasking.* Although commonplace, it can be very stressful for those in this predicament. It's like having one foot on the up escalator and one on the down, being pulled in different directions all day long. Added to this is the pressure of the unrealistic expectation that all jobs must meet the highest standards. For those prone to flipping into Internal Timekeeper mode to multitask, the stress level is high, and so is the cost to their nerves.

Multitasker Caught in Crossfire

Dear Mary and Rene,

My job requires multiple tasks that are all considered to be high priorities. I try to juggle these so that I can accomplish them all. I feel uneasy about which ones to do first and constantly second-guess myself. The result is that I do two or three things at once. I tend to switch direction too often and get to the point where I freeze and become useless. I actually have trouble breathing when this happens and am unable to relax.

I can't concentrate on any one job completely. I'm expected to wrap up everything before I go home, so I run at top speed in order to get all the jobs done. But I always seem to fall behind my schedule, which drives me into a frantic whirlwind of activity. With all these competing demands, work seems to pile up at the end of the day. Recently there has been a physical impact because I've been having chest pains, and this concerns me. When I finally get out of the office, I'm shell-shocked. How do I multitask without being immobilized?"

How to Juggle Jobs Without Dropping the Ball

Dear Shell-Shocked,

Your inability to relax and difficulty breathing sound like a panic reaction. You are assaulted by "input anxiety" and your circuits overload. It's not so much the multitasking per se that's got you in a frenzy; it's the *way* you multitask. You let your attention jump from one project to another without fully concentrating on any. It's a struggle just to keep on top of what you're doing. No wonder you panic.

Multitasking is a new workplace mania. It assumes that if you can do several things at once you are more productive. When you try, you risk losing concentration and sacrificing quality, not to mention your sanity. You're not alone. Our research suggests that being deluged with multiple tasks is a major complaint of the job stressed.

Computers now have multitasking software. Because the computer has a split screen, however, doesn't mean you want a split mind. That's called schizophrenia. Unlike you, the computer doesn't experience stress.

Here are other Internal Timekeeper traits that add to the stress of multi-tasking: You

- Start many tasks at the same time
- Pressure yourself to be in two or more places at once
- Habitually work on several jobs simultaneously

Computer-aided multitasking increases stress because it promotes Internal Timekeeper behavior in those prone to it. Many companies foster the belief in their employees that multitasking allows one person to do the work of four. But even if you juggle four jobs at once, you don't turn into four people. Eventually, the stress goes up and you wear down. Consider this new perception: When you're in four places at once, you're not anywhere at all.

The people who handle multitasking best are organized and concentrated. Neither trait is an Internal Timekeeper strong suit. Instead, random thoughts spray out, attention is easily distracted, ideas are produced then quickly forgotten, and priorities change rapidly, like a bank of flashing neon lights on a Las Vegas casino. Multitasking becomes an ordeal of broken processes and extra work. Very few people can perform this balancing act successfully, and if you have a strong Internal Timekeeper, forget it. You'll soon be a basket case.

To reduce multitasking pressure, read the following stress tips and redirect your Internal Timekeeper's efforts to more productive ends.

STRESS TIPS   A NEW LOOK AT MULTITASKING

Focus on one job at a time.

Focus intently on one job only. Give it your full attention and filter out all other stimulus. This total concentration on the task at hand is a form of meditation. Your mantra could be a cue word to remind Internal Timekeeper to focus. In fact, *focus* would be a good cue word. When you feel your mind drift off and the butterflies start careening around in your innards, do this: Sit down, close your eyes, take a couple of deep breaths, and say to yourself slowly three times, "Focus." If you do this consistently, your body will respond and you will calm down. Then turn your attention to the project at hand. The key is to stay engrossed in what you're doing while you're doing it.

Heed the warning of chest pains.

Get a physical checkup even though Internal Timekeeper insists you don't have time. Chest pains are a serious symptom. If the physician warns you the chest pains are a stress symptom, you've got to learn to think differently about multitasking. Your mind has to rest occasionally. It's unproductive and distressing to mentally inventory all the jobs waiting for you as you try to complete the task at hand. Stick with the job you're doing and put the others out of your mind. The pressure of knowing all those other jobs are waiting increases stress and triggers Internal Timekeeper. You're reminded of still more things

that have to be done. Once turned on, this Stress Personality is hard to turn off, much like Mickey Mouse portraying the Sorcerer's Apprentice in *Fantasia*.

Stress Tips Summary

The suggested stress tips outlined for Shell-shocked will help him get more done in less time by focusing his effort on one thing at a time. Multitasking isn't really about finishing what's started before moving on to something else. It's about concentrating on what you do while you do it. His creativity will be spurred by focused effort, and the quality of his work will improve. Most important, he'll feel back in command of his work flow.

TOPIC SUMMARY

One Head Is Better Than Two

Dear Readers,

Many of you will protest, "But I have to multitask in my job. In fact, I'm evaluated on my ability to do it." Multitasking is a fact of life, it's true, but the crucial point is *how* you multitask. When you observe a smooth and effortless virtuoso multitasker, as in the following example, the Internal Timekeeper style appears chaotic and very stressful by comparison. One day we were late for a meeting at a large hospital. Rushing up to a receptionist in our Internal Timekeeper mode, we asked for directions. She was occupied training a new person. Then her phone rang, and someone called to her from down the hall. It was obvious that we were in a hurry, but she didn't get rattled. She put the caller on hold, sent the trainee off with her lesson, told us she would be with us in a minute, and called an answer down the hall. Although she didn't finish with any one transaction, she was in command of all. Her unhurried and focused manner indicated that Internal Timekeeper didn't come to work with her.

Contrast this with Internal Timekeeper multitasking. Only partial attention is given to everything. Like a water spider skimming around on the surface, the Internal Timekeeper gains no depth or thoroughness. The Internal Timekeeper propensity to drop one job when your attention is diverted causes lost time. When you finally get back to the original task, you've forgotten where you were and have to start all over. To multitask without Internal Timekeeper, get in the habit of taking that extra second or two to make note of where you were when you left off. Flag it, then proceed to your next task and give it your total interest.

Now you're multitasking successfully and managing to keep all those balls in the air. In order to stay balanced on this tightrope, you have to know how to handle interruptions in the three-ring circus that is your day. If you don't, these unexpected intrusions will distract your concentration and topple you from your precarious perch.

STRESSOR TOPIC

HOW TO HANDLE INTERRUPTIONS

Nothing is more frustrating for Internal Timekeeper than interruptions. They are seen as the major stumbling block in trying to get planned work done. People get very upset when they feel the pressure of constant interruptions. They report becoming disorganized, unable to think clearly, inarticulate, curt, abrasive, and angry. As one person in a hurry said to a co-worker, "Get on with it. Just give me the punch line." What they didn't add, but meant, was, "And get the hell out of here and leave me alone." Others report they lose their train of thought when interrupted and have to ask several times that requests be repeated. The following Advice letter describes the feeling of someone who longs to be left alone to plan their day but feels invaded.

Invasion of the Intruders

Dear Mary and Rene,
On my job I'm plagued by constant interruptions from others. These intruders are often rude or rushed, barging in and assaulting me in my

space. They derail my priorities, demanding last-second problem solving to meet their emergencies. I'm never able to bring anything to completion without numerous interruptions. My manager also constantly interrupts me with special projects. Last week, one took two and a half days. Then he asked why my normal work wasn't done. When my phone rings or someone comes into my cube to tell me they need something now, I have a tendency to "lose it." I'm less friendly and may yell or react with a quick angry response. I need to manage this better, especially since handling interruptions is part of my job. The frustration goes home with me and I take it out on my wife and child, which causes more stress. I get headaches and feel tense, nervous, and then irritated at not feeling good. How do I handle interruptions without getting so stressed out?

How to Expect the Unexpected

Dear Invaded,

Your Internal Timekeeper already has you overscheduled before the invasion of the intruders begins. The source of your stress is not so much the interruptions but that you're too tightly scheduled. Since you can't do anything about the interruptions, the only control you have is over how you schedule your time.

Although the interruptions are part of your job description, Internal Timekeeper has you convinced that they are "extra," not a function of your job. That's why you never plan for them. Irritation builds because you're already swamped and now added work keeps pouring in. A new perception is: "Interruptions are not extra work, and time has to be scheduled into my day to accommodate them."

The following Internal Timekeeper traits are spinning your wheels here. You believe that:

- You must be left alone to get your work done.
- Interruptions shouldn't happen.
- If you're crabby and unfriendly, people won't bother you.

You are being influenced by two Stress Personalities. One is Internal Timekeeper, who schedules your time so tightly that there is no flexibility built in to handle the unexpected. Then Sabertooth is recruited to repulse the invaders. They are not really "intruders" since you're paid to help them. It's Sabertooth who applies the label as a rationalization for trying to chase them off. If you work on Internal Timekeeper first and get some sense of how to schedule your time, including time for interruptions, Sabertooth will back off. For some ideas on how to make this balancing act work, read the following stress tips.

STRESS TIPS THE UNEXPECTED IS TO BE EXPECTED

Re-frame your job to fit the reality.

 To reduce the stress of interruptions, you need the following new perception: "Handling interruptions is my job, and my other work has lower priority." Tell your manager that you'll be concentrating on interruptions and that your other work will take a back seat. If necessary, document the amount of time spent on interruptions and get his help to figure out how your time should be allotted. When you accept this, you won't need to bring in Sabertooth to protect you from the "intruders." Another new perception is that "they're colleagues needing my help, and that's my job." Snarling at people won't keep them away, and it makes you less efficient because you lose your concentration.

Set aside a time when you are available to handle interruptions, and let people know when it is.

 To stay in charge of your time, send a clear message to your colleagues that you are not always on call. If they want your help they'll have to do some planning. You can bet that their emergencies are often the result of their Internal Time-keeper disorganization. With someone who always rushes up to you with an SOS emergency job, use the following technique: Before you take on the SOS task of a frantic colleague, ask them to bring you a little more data or information. If they are in a frantic last-minute-emergency mode, many will never come back because they'll either forget or be too impatient to delay. They'll find their own solutions.

You have to protect yourself from Internal Timekeeper, because it is so omnipresent in the workplace. Stand firm and demand adherence to your schedule. When you let people engulf you with last-minute demands, you are rewarding their Internal Timekeeper behavior.

Isolate yourself for a time each day so that you can finish something.

 Arrange your time to insure relief from the interrupters. This will give you a sense of completion, which is necessary for job satisfaction. If you work in an accessible area, put a sign on your desk spelling out when you are available. When people barge in on you, refer to the sign and let them know you'll be happy to help them on schedule. You must develop a sense that you are in control in order to reduce your stress. Prioritize interruptions to stay in control. Obviously, your manager's requests get a higher priority than someone else's. All interrupts are not created equal.

Stress Tips Summary

The theme of all the stress tips for Invaded have to do with taking control of his time. We've suggested a variety of ways. He can isolate himself for a period of the day or build interruptions into his schedule. He can let colleagues know when he's available. He can take charge of each interruption by prioritizing it. The goal is to reduce the sense of being bombarded and assaulted all day long.

TOPIC SUMMARY

Build Interruptions Into Your Workday

Dear Readers,

Many people dread interruptions because of the loss of concentration, which throws them out of whack for the whole day. A stressful perception is that "once I'm interrupted, I have lost concentration and can't regain it." The reason this is so stressful is that the interruptions aren't just momentary. They also disrupt the sense of continuity that keeps you centered. This derails you, and because of Internal Timekeeper it's hard to get back on track. Once you've lost the sense of continuity, the day becomes fragmented. The inability to focus, typical of this Stress Personality, sends you off into a disordered flurry of activity. It seems like you're doing a lot, and you are, but much of it is wasted effort because it is not focused.

Interruptions are normal and a part of every workday. There is no way to avoid them. Yet our research reveals that employees invariably get upset when thrown off schedule. Even those paid to handle them get ticked off by interruptions, mostly because of the Internal Timekeeper stressful perception that a perfect day is one that's interrupt free. What a setup. Since you're never going to have an interruption-free day, you can never have a "perfect" day. A new perception is, "A perfect day is one in which I handle interruptions well," that is, without getting stressed out. Interruptions add to the confusion and stress of your day by keeping you from the work you feel you should be doing. When you can't handle everything, and your work life seems to have gone mad, you feel overwhelmed.

STRESSOR TOPIC

HOW TO AVOID BEING OVERWHELMED AND OVERWROUGHT WHEN OVERWORKED

It's important to recognize when you're stressed out before it incapacitates you. When you're barely hanging on, one more demand can push you over the edge. Add raising children and maintaining a family life, and all your time is spent coping with life rather than enjoying it. You may believe you need Internal Timekeeper to keep you going at a breakneck speed, but you pay a price. For one thing, when you get a reputation as one who gets things done, more work accrues to you. Remember the old adage, "If you want something done, give it to a busy person." Not only do you load yourself down but others see you as a workhorse. If you're barely hanging on now, you've got to curb Internal Timekeeper. You know you've gone too far when you feel constantly overwhelmed, as in the next Advice example.

Man Works Like Dog

Dear Mary and Rene,

For months now I've been working like a dog. Our group has been losing members, but they haven't been replaced. Management keeps taking on more and more customers while expecting us to resolve every question, no matter what it takes. We haven't even heard a thank you from our vice president, who is pushing the whole department. He just wants that bonus. When I'm already doing more than I can handle, someone shows up and demands that I take on yet another task. I react with hostility, stew about it the rest of the day, and catch myself sighing a lot and swearing under my breath.

My upper body is stiff as cement from the tension. Recently I remarked to a friend, "I carry my stress in my neck and shoulders so I'll always know where it is." To make matters worse, I have TMJ, which my dentist says is caused by clenching my teeth while asleep. I've thought about changing jobs; however, prospects elsewhere don't look any better, so I've decided to stick with this one. During my increasingly rare recreation time I feel ashamed about not being productive. Demands at the office mean long hours away from home, and I realize I can't have a work life and home life. If a task cannot be finished during business hours, I have to take it home because it's got to be done.

At work, when phones won't stop ringing, there are three people waiting to see me, ten people have to be called back, and paperwork is piling up on my desk, I get overwhelmed. I have no time for myself and I fantasize about how to escape, but there is no escape. What I'd like you to tell me is, what's going on here? Has the world gone mad, or have I?

Work Life Gone Mad

Dear Gone Mad,

Whether the work world has gone crazy or not, unless you lower your stress, you will. This feeling of being chronically overwhelmed is an Internal Timekeeper stress point. There are several stressful perceptions in your letter that need to be challenged. Here are three of them:

- When you're already doing more than you can handle, you can still take on one more job.
- You can't have a work life and a home life.
- If you take recreation time, you won't be productive.

An obvious self-induced stressor is the nervous way you relax. You feel guilty when you're not working and being productive. This is the worst of options. Although you take the time off, you ruin it with a megadose of self-reproach. Change your perception and tell Internal Timekeeper, "My recreation time is absolutely necessary for me to be productive, and it has to be guilt free." Think of it as a "duty-free" privilege.

Internal Timekeeper has you convinced that you cannot have a home life. To this Stress Personality your survival is attached to working. But what are you working for? Home is a different experience than work, and you need the contrast. Some of your home life has to be devoted to relaxation, fun, and family activities without time pressure. You need to be enriched with contact from your family and to build in periods when there is nothing you have to do. But in order be successful you will have to put the clamps on Internal Timekeeper.

Another stressful perception is, "I can always take on one more job even though my cup 'runneth way over.'" If you wait for Internal Timekeeper to warn you that you're filled to capacity, you'll wait forever. It's not in this Stress Personality's program to limit your activities. So you have to learn to recognize when to say, "No, I can't take on anymore." Otherwise you will continue to let yourself be overwhelmed. The following stress tips will help you set limits on this inner taskmaster.

Choose a time during the afternoon when you stop taking on new jobs.

 Stop taking on anything new after 3 P.M., and focus all your attention on what's already on your plate. You need to put limits on the work flow to keep from feeling overwhelmed. Cut off the intake of new work or you'll be buried in the never-ending avalanche. When you see jobs only coming in and never going out, your anxiety and stress barometer rises. A new perception for you to consider is that no matter how good your intentions, you can never get anything done if you let work keep piling up.

View work as an ongoing process.

 Work is a process much like a stream that is always flowing. By its nature, it's never finished. It was there long before you were born and will be there long after you're dead. You step into the stream and work for a period and then step out and rest. Take breaks, lunch, and vacations and set limits on yourself. Work will be waiting for you the next day. This creates balance and a sense of being in charge of your own destiny. When you feel you have a firm grasp on your life you'll no longer be overwhelmed.

Get a home life free of Internal Timekeeper.

 A new perception is: Home life is not up for grabs. But once you decide to give yourself some "off" time, don't let Internal Timekeeper dictate the quality of that experience. Otherwise you will only transfer doing lists of chores at work to doing the same thing at home. On Saturday morning you'll find yourself saying, "I have to mow the lawn, paint the garage, run to the cleaners, clean the house, take the kids to practice," and on and on until every minute is scheduled. Give yourself at least one of the week-end days to do something recreational. That means no chores of any kind.

Stress Tips Summary

When Gone Mad stops the work flow in the afternoon and concentrates on finishing, his sense of satisfaction will increase. He will view work as an ongoing process and take breaks and rest periods during the day. Finally, he will develop a more balanced home life and start having some fun.

TOPIC  SUMMARY

A Horse of a Different Color

Dear Readers,

Work is not something to be conquered or surmounted. Rather, it's how we all earn our money to finance a life. Included in that life is time for guilt-free recreation and duty-free relaxation. A new perception that is very difficult for Internal Timekeeper to get, but vital, is that you can only do what you can do. You can want to do more, other people can want you to do more, you can work like a speed demon, you can feel guilty if you're not always productive, but in the end there is only so much you can do. The difference in your quality of life is whether you do this full of stress or with some sense of fulfillment.

In order to get yourself some free time, you have to say no to excessive demands. Like Striver and Pleaser, Internal Timekeeper will prevent you from saying no when you need to. Pleaser's motive is to avoid making others unhappy. Striver assumes the burden of responsibility because of the belief that only you can do things right. Internal Timekeeper's rationale is, "Oh well, one more job won't hurt, and I don't have time to say no anyway." So off you go in a cloud of dust, and work collects or accumulates like lint on wool clothing. A new perception for this Stress Personality is: There is always less you could do. To handle Internal Timekeeper, your efforts have to go toward reducing the amount of activity in your life. That means both on the job and off.

A Busy Mind Creates a Chaotic Life

Dear Readers,

Internal Timekeeper behavior is reinforced in our culture. It starts when we're little children. Remember when one of your parents walked into the room and caught you daydreaming? "What's the matter, haven't you got something to do? If you can't find anything to do, I'll find something for you." Of course, that usually meant chores, so you quickly dashed out of earshot. In the Army, sergeants bark, "Do something, even if it's wrong." And many times bosses say seriously, "You should always look busy, because customers like to buy from an establishment that looks busy." Yet we've heard hundreds of people in our workshops tell us, "I won't stand in line for anything. I buy my groceries at a Seven Eleven rather than have to wait at a busy place."

Is "Too Much to Do" Perception or Reality?

Is there really too much to do all the time, or is it that Internal Timekeeper always sees a world with too much to do? The answer is both. When you tell yourself constantly that there's too much to do, you feel overwhelmed. It's true that work involves endless tasks that must be completed. But if you view work as a "stream" that's always there, you can reduce stress by regarding it as just what you do while at the office. It's not too much or too little. It's true that companies put more pressure on employees and there are fewer of you expected to do more work. But you still can only do as much as you can do.

Employees are feeling the effects of corporate Internal Timekeeper policies and complaining about the pressure. Notice that in the last advice letter, Gone Mad lamented the fact that though the department had worked so hard, the vice president didn't thank them. This is a clue that the vice president most likely doesn't think there's anything to thank them for. It's their job. What would happen if the VP did thank them? Would they work harder? Would they feel better? If so, what Gone Mad is saying is that if he got gratitude and praise for working so hard, he'd work even harder. Yet he already admits to working as hard as he can and is overwhelmed. What all this means is you have to recognize how your Internal Timekeeper makes you vulnerable to these corporate policies. Once you do, you can choose to change the way you react to Internal Timekeeper pressure.

Prisoners of Time

We've long heard people lament that they'd like to get away from the office at a reasonable hour, "But there's so much do, I just can't seem to get out of there." A similar complaint comes from people who don't take vacations. "If I go on vacation, there will be so much work piled up waiting for me, I'll never catch up. So why leave?" What both arguments have in common is an acknowledgment that you can be enslaved by the tyranny of all the work there is to be done.

So how do you escape this self-imposed prison? First you have to reassure your Internal Timekeeper that it's OK to leave even though there's still lots to be done. There will always be lots to be done. A change in attitude is essential. A single mother is unable to tear herself away from work prior to her blessed event. Then she has a baby and—presto!—she finds a way to leave at 5:30 P.M. because she has to pick up her child at daycare. What was a big problem becomes a non-issue because she's had a change in perspective. Her new perception becomes, "I have no choice; I have to take care of my child."

When you work ceaselessly, there's no allowance for unplanned time so that life can happen to you. Serendipity sometimes presents us with wonderful, unexpected joys. All work and no play erases the mystery of life. It also interferes with creativity. You become too busy for the time to think or explore new ideas, so you recycle the same old ones because it's quicker. Bringing Internal Timekeeper into closer scrutiny will help you rein this wild horse in.

When you notice yourself dashing around in a big rush, ask yourself, "What's the hurry?" Periodically during the day say to your Internal Timekeeper, "Slow down." It can be your Internal Timekeeper mantra. Do it every time you catch yourself in a mad dash. Life is speeding by fast enough as it is. Why hurry it along?

QUICK-REFERENCE STRESS TIPS FOR _INTERNAL TIMEKEEPER_

To remind yourself to slow down during your frenetic day, refer to these stress tips:

- Prioritize your work and limit your "To Do" list.
- Allot a specific amount of time to each task.
- Build interruptions into your day.
- Slow down and stop overscheduling.
- View interruptions as normal business, not intrusions.
- Cut new work off at 3 P.M. and use the rest of the day to finish things.
- Reduce the number of activities to allow focus and creativity.
- Concentrate on one task at a time.
- Allocate time on your daily "To Do" list for emergencies.
- View work as an ongoing process.

Sabertooth

The World Is a Dog-Eat-Dog Place

How to Recognize *Sabertooth*

Tom sits at his desk deep in thought about the budget for the new fiscal year. He's on a tight schedule and can't afford distractions. Out of the corner of his eye he notices a subordinate, Martin, hovering in the doorway, trying to catch his attention. Tom quickly returns to his work but feels a surge of anger as he mutters to himself, "If this guy interrupts me once more about some damn piddling detail, I'm going to throttle him. I'll ignore him and maybe he'll go away." No such luck. Martin fidgets as he waits for acknowledgment, and his anxiousness radiates across the room, enveloping Tom. Looking up, Tom asks sharply, "What the hell do you want this time?" "Just a quick look at these figures," Martin explains nervously. "They don't seem right to me and . . ." Tom's face reddens as he glares at Martin and growls, "Can't you see I'm busy?"

Tom is well aware he has a short fuse and hates to lose his temper, as happened this morning at a management meeting. Two managers who always try to maneuver complex pieces of work into his group were at it again. They use the excuse that Tom's inventory control coordinator has a lot of specialized expertise. This makes his group a choice target of these finaglers. Once again he was forced to fight a battle to protect his group. He had wanted the meeting to go smoothly this time, but his dislike and mistrust of the schemer of the moment aroused his anger, and he was loathe to cooperate. As a familiar feeling of stubborn resistance welled up in him, he let loose some choice, hostile, sarcastic remarks. The meeting ended with an air of unresolved tension and bad feeling.

Furthermore, he learned yesterday from a well-meaning colleague that some of these same managers were talking behind his back, questioning his competency. This added to his aggravation, and revenge fantasies began dancing in his head. He's startled out of his vengeful plotting when he hears Martin clear his throat: "Ah, oh, excuse me." Fuming, Tom stares at his subordinate, and realizes how tempted he is to let out all his pent-up anger at the unsuspecting and innocent Martin. Tom's Sabertooth is on the warpath today.

How *Sabertooth* Causes Stress

It's normal to get angry but important how you express it. Sabertooth anger is stress provoking because it reacts like nuclear fission. As you let the pent-up anger out, it triggers still more rage and builds until you're ready to explode. Old grudges that were never settled can set off this response. Sabertooth keeps your nerves on a prickly edge. You're perpetually on guard against people you fear will manipulate you. Under the pressure of work overload and the stress of too many demands, Sabertooth free-floating hostility is easily set off. Since it's not attached to anyone or anything in particular, you go around mad at nothing and everything. It can be ignited by daily stress. When aroused, Sabertooth will look for a target to legitimize the feeling. Once you've come up with a reason, the anger feeds on itself and keeps you in a state of uneasy belligerence.

Advice to the Job Stressed

Sabertooth stress, and the resultant fallout on bosses, subordinates, peers, loved ones, and strangers is featured in the Advice examples in this chapter. In the first, "Buried in the Graveyard Shift," an angry subordinate is certain her boss doesn't respect her opinions and is thwarting her career. The advice suggests some effective ways to let go of needless anger and refocus actions to promote career growth.

The next situation, "Angry Negotiator Complains of Spousal Enthusiasm Abuse," moves to the home front. A weary contract negotiator, who yearns for quiet to unwind from a grueling day, engages in a cold war with his wife. Stress tips provide new rules for engagement to satisfy the needs of both.

THE *SABERTOOTH* STRESS TEST

Read the questions below and place a check (✓) in the appropriate column to the right to indicate your response. Find out how your Sabertooth beliefs and behaviors increase your stress. Pay attention to the questions you checked "Usually" and "Frequently." These have to be reduced to "Occasionally" or "Seldom" in order to control Sabertooth.	NEVER	SELDOM	OCCASIONALLY	FREQUENTLY	USUALLY
Do I: 1. Fear others will try to manipulate me if they can? 2. Respond to slights with tit for tat? 3. Become unyielding, stubborn, or rigid when disagreed with? 4. React with anger and hostility in conflict? 5. Believe the world is full of sharks? 6. Attack to prevent others from taking advantage of me? 7. Become angry, argumentative, and defensive when challenged? 8. Feel angry and insulted when I suspect I've been betrayed? 9. Take my temper out on loved ones? 10. Become short, curt, and sarcastic when under stress?					

Commuter stress is the subject of "Auto Erratic Behavior." Angry freeway follies make for a stressful commute to and from work as Sabertooth gets behind the wheel. How to smooth the journey is the driving lesson for stressed-out commuters. In the last Advice example, conflict splinters a work group into factions. In "The Flag Bearer," Joan of Arc picks up the flag, leads the charge, and discovers that her troops have deserted. Rallying the support of co-workers who share her views sends "Flag Bearer" marching to a different drummer.

Read the "Dear Mary and Rene" letters. The replies to these letters will provide you with tips designed to cool off Sabertooth.

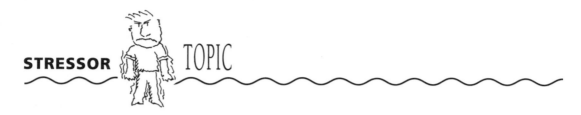

STRESSOR TOPIC

HOW TO LET GO OF NEEDLESS ANGER

It takes a great deal of energy to marshal your forces for an attack on what could be an imaginary enemy. It could also be a career-limiting move (CLM). Sabertooth, ever vigilant for assaults on your competence, easily jumps to conclusions regarding the motives of others. When a manager's conduct is construed as a threat to your career advancement, Sabertooth steps forward. This part of you becomes the interpreter of the manager's motives. In the following Advice example, an angry subordinate learns to use a less bellicose strategy to cope with an indifferent manager.

Buried in the Graveyard Shift

Dear Mary and Rene,

My direct manager assigned me the task of documenting and finding solutions to obstructions in our department that are slowing response time. Yet when I make suggestions she dismisses them or says, "I've already thought of that." When she does this I feel tricked and demeaned. I've worked hard on this project, brainstorming ideas, identifying the trouble spots, and trying to get people to change procedures. I get short fused and sometimes yell at those who keep screwing things up. But no one seems to care or take me seriously. One lead worker told me to "lighten up" because these problems will never be solved anyway as the manager doesn't want to be bothered. But I still feel responsible.

For the last two weeks I've been assigned the graveyard shift, ostensibly to identify bottlenecks. However, I fear that the manager means to bury me there because she thinks I'm causing her too many headaches. I feel she's betrayed and manipulated me. I get so angry I want to attack and force her to deal with me. It's affecting my love life as I tend to vent my anger at my fiancé even though he sympathizes with me. How do I get taken seriously without getting angry?

The Sabertooth Interpretation

Dear Buried,

No wonder you feel so incensed and disregarded. You're buying Sabertooth's version of this clash of expectations. According to Sabertooth, the manager purposely tricked and manipulated you. First you're assigned to help identify and fix functional breakdowns. So you, in good faith, go to a lot of trouble, including changing to the night shift, to carry out the job. Then you hear from a third person that the manager was never really serious about solving these problems. "The reason she exiled you to the night shift was to get you out of sight and out of her hair," says Sabertooth. "If she thinks she's going get away with this, she's tangled with the wrong person." Here are some of the Sabertooth stressful perceptions that are digging you in deeper:

■ You are being manipulated and betrayed.

■ If you get angry enough others will have to deal with you.

■ If your ideas aren't accepted you're being dismissed.

When your Sabertooth tells you that you're being toyed with, it's bound to raise your hackles. A new perception is that your manager's disinterest in your ideas has more to do with her than you. Taking things too personally is a Sabertooth sore point, and leads to ascribing malicious intent in unclear circumstances. It's possible your boss is overwhelmed and can't handle making changes. There could be many reasons your manager doesn't want to be bothered other than your alleged ineffectiveness at finding solutions she desires. Sabertooth's interpretation of her motivation is your stressor. The following stress tips will help you shift your position and release you from all this anger.

To let go of your anger, reinterpret the cause.

 Always question Sabertooth's interpretation. It will be tinged with paranoia. Maybe you're being shunted off because your manager doesn't want to deal with all your anger, and it has nothing to do with your ideas. Many managers avoid conflict and recoil from angry subordinates because they don't know how to deal with them.

Present your ideas for change as thoroughly and effectively as you can. If your manager doesn't act on them, move on to something else and know you've done your job. No amount of rage and fury is going to intimidate your manager into feeling joyful acceptance if she doesn't want to. It only raises your stress and alienates you from others.

Don't shout to be heard.

 Stand up for yourself and voice your opinions without being antagonistic. You can get more with pleasant persuasion than with hostility and vengeance. It's a Sabertooth stressful perception that if you yell loud enough you'll be heard. However, much like children who are always being yelled at, colleagues eventually turn off their ears and don't listen. Assume you are being heard when you talk in a calm and rational manner. Ask for feedback and give the other person plenty of opportunity to participate. Use sentences like, "I'd be interested to know what you have to say," or "Tell me more about that subject." Sabertooth conversations are often too loud and one-sided. You want to do whatever is necessary to encourage two-way communication. Bellowing won't get you there.

Don't personalize manager-subordinate exchanges.

 Sabertooth is convinced your manager's treatment of you is a personal attack on your competency and, by extension, you. You're being asked to find bottlenecks and solutions. Do the best job you can and your competency can never be an issue to yourself. You were assigned the task in the first place because of your skill. Presume it was because your manager had confidence in you. Go ahead and do your job, but heed the well-meaning advice of the lead worker to "lighten up."

Stress Tips Summary

These stress tips will give Buried another way to handle this episode. Without Sabertooth's prodding, she can expand her strategic options. If she is being manipulated she needs a clear head to maneuver her way out of the graveyard. She doesn't want to be stuck there. The tips of creating two-way communication, not taking things personally, and reacting in a calm, less belligerent manner will uncover the manager's hidden agenda, if there is one. And either Buried has a problem she needs to resolve or she exaggerated the whole episode and can dismiss it.

TOPIC  SUMMARY

Who's Manipulating Whom?

Dear Readers,

Nobody can really manipulate you unless you let them. Sabertooth clouds and narrows your vision with fury so that you don't see any other alternative except warfare. Creative solutions are lost and you feel you have no control, a fearsome prospect for Sabertooth. The tension builds because Sabertooth believes people want to take advantage of you by trying to control your life. To prevent this, Sabertooth says, "We have to be in control at all times."

Manifestations of this are the exasperating Sabertooth qualities of always having the last word and insisting on being right. A new perception is that it's a sign of strength to trust.

This Stress Personality sees its role as protecting you from perceived attacks. The idea is to make you tough, invulnerable, self-reliant, aggressive, successful, and no one to trifle with. When someone takes advantage anyway, you're left with a sense of betrayal that is bound to be hurtful. These feelings alert Sabertooth that you need protection, and this Stress Personality swings into action. Now you have to deal with two stressors: your hurt feelings and Sabertooth's response. It's better to reinterpret events so you don't feel hurt. Then Sabertooth won't need to rush to the rescue.

A new perception is that most people aren't out to get you. They're too busy. They are just trying to survive and have little interest in hatching conspiracies to make your life miserable. It's not only managers at work who pose a threat to your autonomy, according to Sabertooth. You have to be alert even with family and loved ones, as in the following Advice example.

STRESSOR TOPIC

HOW TO GET SPACE FROM YOUR SPOUSE

In our research, people lament that they have no time to themselves to unwind. The general complaint is, "I never have any quiet time just for me." Very often Sabertooth is the behavior, not necessarily of choice, that emerges in an attempt to make a clearing of tranquillity. With longer work hours and more job stress, the need for a sanctuary of quiet to unwind from grueling days is essential. Sabertooth is used by many people to get distance from pressure and intrusions. But the Sabertooth method of gaining solitude, clamming up and shutting others out, doesn't serve the purpose. Instead, it stirs up uneasiness and rancor. The following Advice case illustrates a common Sabertooth problem: getting crabby when feeling crowded.

Angry Negotiator Complains of Spousal Enthusiasm Abuse

Dear Mary and Rene,
Every evening when I get home from work, my affectionate, caring spouse talks my head off when what I really need is quiet. She says

she can't control herself because she's "just that way." I pretend I'm listening, say nothing, and wait for her to finish. When she doesn't stop in my time frame, I shut her up with all kinds of body language cues. I refuse to look her in the eye, display disinterest, and sometimes walk away while she's talking. Then I might pick up the newspaper and start to read. The more she talks, the more irritable I become. I just don't answer. When I feel myself start to boil over at her yakking, I become distant and cold and avoid close contact. I often like to talk and listen to her, but not when I'm forced to. How do I get my wife to leave me alone so I can get the peace and quiet I need to unwind from the day?

Shutting Out Talkative Wife Backfires

Dear Abused,

You sound like a victim of "enthusiasm abuse." No, it's not a new syndrome; it's your Sabertooth viewing affectionate enthusiasm from your wife as an attack. You say you're "forced" to engage in this unwanted interaction. You feel forced because you're not dealing with the relationship clash in a direct, open manner. Instead, you're using Sabertooth body language to ward her off. When you push her away and close her out when she wants intimacy, her anxiety is triggered and she talks more than ever. In fact, she probably grabs you the second you step in the door because she's afraid you'll clam up, close off, and disappear before she's had any chance at all to make contact.

You are contributing to the stress of this domestic squabble with the following Sabertooth reactions:

- Indirect communication and dismissive body language
- Withholding warm and tender feelings when feeling threatened
- Clamming up, pouting, and freezing out people when you're angry

When you turn into iceman, your wife tries harder to melt your defenses. The Sabertooth characteristics of pouting, clamming up, and freezing out are ploys to both control the other person and get space for yourself. The drawback is that they are too indirect. Others often don't know what you're doing even though they experience the chill. A new perception for your Sabertooth is, "The more direct I am without anger, the less I'll have to distance."

If your spouse is coming from Pleaser, your behavior will seem to her like punishment, and she'll do everything in her power to get back in your good graces. The more you shut her out with Sabertooth, the more she'll be pounding on the door to get in. This is the opposite of what you say you need when you get home, which is distance and quiet. The following stress tips will show you how frank, open discussion can bring you out of cold storage and warm up your relationship.

STRESS TIPS   NEGOTIATING SPACE BRINGS RAPPROCHEMENT

Negotiate and create the space you need in your relationship.

 When your Sabertooth feels "forced" into anything you immediately dig in your heels and become stubborn. A new perception is that there is no way you can be forced to communicate against your will. By its nature, communication is a two-way street and so is a relationship. There is *you* and there is *her* which make up, *us*. Sounds like you're afraid of losing *you* to *her* and having *us* take up the whole space. Talk to her about your concerns. You might say something like, "Honey, when I first walk in the door I'm not my most social or available." Tell her what time you will be, and keep that date. That way she knows she can have some contact and attention and you will still control your own space. Sabertooth will feel less threatened and go off duty because you are taking care of yourself.

Consider your wife's needs.

 A new perception for you to apply is, "Mine are not the only needs that have to be satisfied in this relationship." Try to understand more about what it really is your spouse wants from you. "Yakking" does not sound like a very satisfying connection for either of you. People have many different motives for conversation and also many different styles. Sabertooth tends toward terse statements like "Get to the point."

Your wife may use conversation to stay connected and feel intimate. For her, the communicating itself may be more important than the content of what she says, but you interpret it as "yakking" and dismiss it because all you hear is words. Re-label her "yakking" as something more inviting, like "connecting."

Question her declaration that she can't control herself, that she's "just that way."

 As part of your negotiation, bring this up in a pleasant and assertive way. Healthy relationships require compromise. Make it clear to her it's not OK to be "just that way." If her behavior affects your relationship negatively, it's the responsibility of both to negotiate a satisfactory solution. Offer to make some changes of your own that will satisfy her. For example, you could agree to be available for fifteen minutes of instant intimacy on those evenings she designates as really important. Later, when you've wound down, be more available to listen. Get a contract with her that when you say, "Not tonight dear, it's been one of those days," she holds off talking until you're available. Compromise is the glue that holds a relationship together, and Sabertooth especially needs practice at this.

Stress Tips Summary

When Abused stops feeling like a victim of his wife's loquaciousness and in a friendly, pleasant way asserts his need for space, it's more likely she will listen to him. He will no longer have to punish her with Sabertooth in order to get space.

TOPIC SUMMARY

Sabertooth, Purr Like a Kitten

Dear Readers,

A lot of people verbalize the faulty perception, "I was born this way and can never change." When Sabertooth encounters an unwillingness on the part of the other person to modify their attitude, a test of wills results. The "I am what I am" pronouncement is itself a Sabertooth attitude. Implied in the statement is resistance that stems from an unwillingness to compromise. Then you have a Sabertooth versus Sabertooth quarrel, and relationship fireworks are sure to follow.

A different form of fireworks can be expected in the Sabertooth-Pleaser relationship. Because it's so common, the dynamics of that relationship can be very stressful if the protagonists aren't aware of what's going on. The attraction of Sabertooth-Pleaser is symbiotic. Sabertooth aggressiveness often balances the passivity of the Pleaser-dominated partner. After the Sabertooth partner's explosion at friend, family, or foe, Pleaser energy is useful in patching up hurt feelings and wounded sensibilities.

But the pitfalls of this relationship are contained in the Pleaser need to always be in the circle of love and the Sabertooth need for distance and autonomy. One mission of your Sabertooth is to guard against letting yourself be vulnerable. For many people it results in a hard shell of protective rigidity. In a relationship this armor can make you too difficult for others to know and hence bother with. Contrary to what Sabertooth believes, you can't experience love in its totality without revealing yourself. This means a willingness to be vulnerable. The next time you are aware of feeling irritated about something, tell the other person about the emotion without angry words. This is not a position of weakness but one of strength, and this is especially true in a personal relationship.

Sabertooth can stir you into outrage at anyone. In the first Advice letters, the "enemy" was the manager; in the second, a spouse. In the next, Sabertooth targets a perfect stranger.

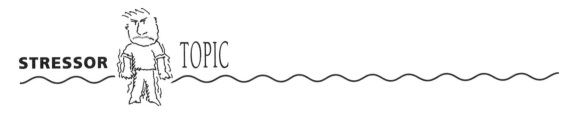

STRESSOR TOPIC

HOW TO HANDLE COMMUTE STRESS

Strange things are happening on the nation's highways. In a freeway frenzy, commuters are taking out their stress on each other and are exhibiting "auto erratic" stress behavior. Tailgating, cutting in too close for comfort, chasing each other, shouting obscenities, and flipping the bird are typical examples. Newspapers carry accounts of gunplay between angry and frustrated commuters. Even the most mild-mannered drivers erupt into violent reactions at real or imagined insults from other drivers, as the following example shows.

Auto Erratic Behavior

Dear Mary and Rene,

I have a two-hour drive into work each day, which causes me stress. Everything from rudeness of other drivers to serious misjudgments gets my blood pressure soaring. Sometimes I drive aggressively, and sometimes I drive slow just to get a rise out of people. When I'm hurrying to work I notice my teeth are clenched; I'm uptight, anxious, and angry. I talk out loud at other commuters, gesturing and swearing.

When some idiot in the fast lane blocks me, I blink my headlights and curse at them to get over. The other day a lady cut in front of me for no reason. So I passed her, got in front of her, and slowed way down. Guess what she did? She passed me in the fast lane, gave me the finger, and tried to squeeze me into a truck in the lane to my right. I thought, "This lady must be crazy." I realized I could follow her home and beat her up. Not that I would, but there are enough weirdos on the freeway who might. She must have decided the same thing, because she immediately exited. The insanity of my uncharacteristic reaction unnerved me. My question is, why do I get so mad at flaky drivers?

Who Are You Really Mad At?

Dear Auto Erratic,

It's possible that displaced anger is one of the causes of your Sabertooth driving behavior. People muffle angry feelings at bosses, co-workers, and subordinates and blow them off at strangers while driving home. Others are angry at the conditions they work under and feel helpless to do anything about them.

People who are normally mild mannered climb into the powerful steel capsules that are their cars and allow themselves to react in ways they would never think of in other circumstances. They are depersonalized and have anonymity. It's similar to "flaming" e-mail. One can spew out all the invective built up in a day without having to take responsibility for it, because you don't have to face the target. Sabertooth stressful perceptions that make your commute a war zone include the following:

- Drivers are deliberately provoking you.
- Rude commuters have to be paid back for their flaky driving.
- Angry gestures and yelling will teach others to be safe drivers.

Don't be so hard on your fellow commuters. It's not worth the stress. A new perception that will help to calm you down is that people aren't tormenting you on purpose. Many are unaware of what's going on around them and only seem to be indifferent or reckless. When the lady cut in front of you, it would have been much less stressful to let her go and give her no energy. When you encountered another Sabertooth, which you obviously did, you engaged in freeway roulette, a very dangerous game. Freeways are risky enough without waving red flags in front of tired, irritated, frustrated, and frazzled commuters. The following stress tips will suggest more tranquil driving habits and bring down that soaring blood pressure.

STRESS TIPS PUTTING ON THE BRAKES

Leave the driving lessons to traffic school.

Resist your Sabertooth's tendency to teach others a lesson with a new perception: It's not your obligation to teach others how to drive. Your only responsibility is to get yourself to work and return home safely. Drive defensively. Don't engage other crazy drivers; stay away from them. You don't want to get so irate that you also become a road menace. Listen to soothing music or books on tape. Non-auto erratic drivers say that their commute is cherished as a way to wind down. Some use the drive as a quiet period for thought, perhaps the only time they'll get for themselves the whole day. Don't ruin this interlude by chasing around after errant drivers to prove you're "right." You may be right, and you also may be dead right.

Temper your hot head when in your hot rod.

Cool down and chill out. Don't leave the driving to Sabertooth; it's hazardous to your health and not worth the soaring blood pressure. When you get so keyed up and angry, it triggers the flight-or-fight response. This powerful physiological reaction is produced by a surge of adrenaline to prepare for aggressive action or rapid flight. There is no question that driving to work on crowded freeways is stressful, but it's not the same as facing a Sabertooth cat. However, our bodies don't know the difference. A driving examiner for the Oregon Department of Transportation told us an interesting fact. Studies of drivers in heavy commuter traffic reveal that they have higher stress levels than astronauts sitting in a capsule on the end of a booster rocket about to be sent into space.

Stress Tips Summary

When Auto Erratic accepts the new perception that he cannot improve other drivers by screaming at them, he'll have a more objective perspective. He'll learn to take a closer look at his anger and leave it at work instead of commuting with it.

TOPIC SUMMARY

A Peaceful Commute Brings Stress Relief

Dear Readers,

Sabertooth bursts of rage can be serious and are never well thought out. Had Auto Erratic followed his Sabertooth impulse to chase the woman and beat her up, look at all the trouble he would have gotten into. Another participant of our workshops, who considered himself a calm and rational person, got so provoked at a motorist who nearly caused him an accident that he jumped out of his car at the stoplight, ran up to her, and pounded on her window. "I was furious and started to give her a lecture. She rolled the window down a short way, looked at me, and said, 'You must have a terrible life.' I was speechless. She stopped me cold. Looking back on it I realized she was right. I was angry at my work frustrations and dumping it on this lady."

People act out their frustrations on the freeways for a number of different reasons. Most of those polled in our programs did so because of an unusual stressful perception. They believed that by honking, gesturing, and yelling at the offending driver they could teach him or her a lesson—the lesson being good road habits, which will make the freeway a safer place. They were under the illusion that one outraged gesture could permanently modify the errors of bad drivers. "I can make the person aware of the fact that she or he is driv-ing poorly, and they will improve with my help," is the reasoning.

To demonstrate how faulty this perception is, ask yourself how you react to a raging motorist who comes roaring up to you, neck veins pulsating, waving their arms and shouting something you can't hear. Do you believe that makes you a better driver?

There are more people commuting over longer distances in heavier traffic, so it's important that you minimize the stress. A helpful new perception is that you are a professional driver. Recently, we observed the professionalism of a hotel limousine operator in Los Angeles. When a car entered our lane at high speed and cut him off, he slowed down, safely changed lanes, and continued chatting pleasantly as if nothing had happened. When we commented on his coolness he replied, "I can't afford to get hot over things like that. I'm a professional." Consider yourself a professional driver, and you'll drive more safely because you won't personalize the blunders of your fellow commuters.

Sabertooth can present many faces. The take-charge attitude can change focus from the freeway to your work group. In the following example, Sabertooth assumes the mantle of leadership for a work group intimidated by a strong and aggressive colleague.

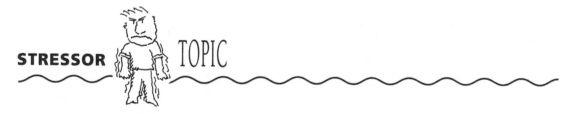

STRESSOR TOPIC

HOW TO HANDLE CO-WORKERS IN CONFLICT

A conflict between co-workers can be a ticklish affair. Since the relationship is theoretically equal, a quick retreat into the role of boss to settle things is unavailable. When the conflict involves a whole work group, frequently one or two antagonists emerge. One decides to take on the other in the name of saving the group. This "Joan of Arc" role can be played by either male or female. It goes like this: The group gets up in arms over some hot issue. They implore or convince an outspoken member who agrees with their cause to pick up the flag and lead them into battle. As you will learn in the next letter, the "Flag Bearer" ends up being not only the first one shot but the only target.

The Flag Bearer

Dear Mary and Rene,

I'm in a very stressful position, and it's causing great turmoil in the quality of my work and home life. I'm having a conflict with a co-worker who's buddies with the manager and who wants to be our lead. I don't like this guy, nor does anyone else in the group. He's aloof, won't acknowledge greetings, and holes up in his office with the doors closed and lights low. If disturbed, he lashes out at everyone. He and I clashed over a choice for an off-site team-building session.

He tried to cram his selection down our throats by e-mail, without any consideration for the rest of us. Everybody came to me upset, saying, "Somebody should do something about this guy; he's already starting to act like the lead." I realized I had to take him on because I'm the most out-spoken. Also, I was furious with him and was determined not to let him get away with bossing us around. It all came to a head when the manager called a meeting and this guy lied about trying to dictate the choice of the off-site. I challenged him in front of the manager and said, "The e-mail you sent us and what you are saying now are quite different, as the rest of group will verify. Isn't that right, group?" There was complete silence. My words hung in the air like a puff of cannon smoke, and I was shot down. As I lay bleeding on the table, no one came to my rescue. They sat looking at their shoes. Not one of the people who complained to me spoke up. I was mortified and furious and vowed to myself never to get out on a limb again. As I'm a very proactive person, this option is not palatable. How can I get the group to speak up and support me?

A Call to Arms

Dear Flag Bearer,

Although it was noble of you to take on the irascible would-be leader, the outcome was predictable. You were dealing with a Sabertooth and responding from your Sabertooth but were followed by an army of

Pleasers. The first mistake you made was to agree to be their mouth-piece. It's typical in a conflict for people to react with an exasperating Pleaser characteristic, which is to fan the fires of discontent in private, find a proactive soldier like you, then dive into the trenches when the shooting starts.

This setup will enrage your Sabertooth. You were exposed and embarrassed in front of your manager. Furthermore, it accomplished nothing. Now the manager is probably convinced that your antagonist should be appointed lead, since obviously nobody else is leading. To see how your Sabertooth lured you into this ambush, consider the following stressful perceptions driving your behavior. You believe:

- Because you're outspoken, you're the one to take the risk.
- Since the co-workers are so upset, they will back you.
- If the manager knows what's really going on, he'll side with you.

Your Sabertooth apparently ignored the fact that the manager and your adversary were "buddies." At the least this suggests that he's going to get the boss's ear more often than you. This means you need to be doubly prepared with reinforcements, because you're at a disadvantage. Prudence dictates that when you're about to try something risky, have your ammunition ready before confrontation. Since your colleagues are reacting with Pleaser, they will be fearful of speaking up to the authority figure, especially one whose dander is up.

Write down your colleagues' complaints, and if they don't speak up, you present them in the meetings so all they have to do is acknowledge, "Yes, I did say that." A new perception to consider is that by not carrying the flag yourself, you are giving others the opportunity to do so. The following stress tips will help you march to a different drummer.

Refuse to be spokesperson unless others show willingness to speak up.

Speak privately to the people who left you bloody on the table. Tell them you are very disappointed in their nonsupport and will no longer be the spokesperson. Obviously you can't force others to be more assertive and step forward when called upon. But you can let each person know that at the meeting you will be repeating what they said to you in private. Let them take the responsibility for dealing with whatever flak they get from the would-be lead. If they are not willing to have what they said to you privately made public, refuse to listen to the complaints. They are using you instead of taking assertive action themselves.

Assertively seek the lead job yourself.

If you decide you want to stay in this group, you could try for the lead job. It sounds like you are a natural leader. Organize your Pleaser army. Instead of being just a conduit for complaints, use that proactive energy to mobilize the group. How can you utilize their support and confidence in you? Your Pleaser troops will be more comfortable with indirect action. Perhaps e-mail to the manager recommending you for the position would work.

Don't get into a conflict or contest with your antagonist. Turn your manager into an ally by soliciting his suggestions as to how you could advance your career in this setting. Overwhelm him with competence. But avoid forcing him to make a "me or him" choice between you and his buddy.

Keep your options and the back door open.

Since you are such a proactive person, this might not be the right environment for you. Evaluate this altercation from a non-Sabertooth perspective. You are outnumbered, outflanked, and without support from your timid co-workers. Sabertooth will insist that you stubbornly dig in and keep fighting. However, there are times when the best and smartest assertive act is to retreat. The concept of retreat is not always synonymous with defeat.

In the darkest days of the Korean War, when United Nations troops were reeling under heavy attack and forced to retreat from the Chosin Reservoir, American general O.P. Smith defiantly proclaimed that his troops weren't retreating, but merely advancing in another direction. Within a few months, the same troops were back on the attack and regained all their lost ground. So spruce up your resume and start looking for other options. Your Sabertooth will simmer down knowing that you are in control of your stay or leave options.

Stress Tips Summary

The stress tips for Flag Bearer provide options that will keep Sabertooth from feeling trapped. She will refuse to be spokesperson unless others are willing to take responsibility. She can either seek the lead job for herself or retreat and wait for a more auspicious time.

TOPIC  SUMMARY

Rally Round the Flag

Dear Readers,

When you control Sabertooth, your energy can be directed toward resolving disagreements and planning strategy when in conflict. Instead of reacting impulsively, you can be coolly objective. Always look for a new perception to apply. There are various possibilities for dealing with any dispute that you haven't thought of before. Fewer options are available when you're stuck in an adversarial frame of mind. Can you see the conflict in a different light? Look for ways to compromise. It's also important to be willing to admit when you're wrong. It's a sign of strength and fosters people's confidence in you.

A Sabertooth versus Sabertooth clash can be very destructive. Deadlock is the result, and the reason for the conflict is shelved and never addressed. All the intensity goes into a struggle over who's going to win. The struggle can't be resolved because it's become a personality clash. Sabertooth is not a reliable position to assume in a workplace conflict where compromise is essential.

POSTSCRIPT

Soothing the Savage Beast Within

Dear Readers,

Not only is Sabertooth hard on other people, it can be detrimental to your health. Research into heart disease implicates Sabertooth-type anger as a serious risk factor. This kind of anger includes the nuclear fission reaction referred to earlier. Anger stimulates ever-increasing levels of rage, prolonging the agitation in your body over time, and can become a chronic condition. Free-floating hostility is one manifestation. That's why holding grudges is particularly hazardous. A grudge acts like a software bug that periodically triggers the memory of an old insult, slight, or affront. Every time you think of the original instance, the anger surges and can easily inflame your entire disposition.

Another serious manifestation of Sabertooth stress is "overkill" anger. This is the habit of blowing a trivial incident into a volcanic explosion of rage. It needlessly revs your cardiovascular system into red alert, which is hard enough on you when the threat is real. But if they occur over and over in response to minor issues, these explosions can increase your chances of becoming a heart attack victim.

Life Imitates Art

The main character in Arthur Miller's play *Death of a Salesman* is Willy Loman, a prototype of Sabertooth. He is aggressive, opinionated, rigid, and prone to outbursts over the alleged abuses he receives from the world at large. We once met his incarnation, a salesman for seminars sponsored by the Silicon Valley Chamber of Commerce. He was assigned to sell our stress program, which was set up for two consecutive evenings.

Our "Willy" was in his mid fifties but looked older. His skin had a gray pallor, and the dark circles under his eyes gave him a worn-out look.

During a breakfast meeting the day of the first evening seminar, he told us, "Well, my doc says I have to reduce my stress because I got a problem with the old ticker." He went on, "But hell, stress goes with the territory." Recognizing his Sabertooth early on, we couldn't resist giving him several suggestions as to how to reduce his Sabertooth stress, all of which he rejected. We also warned him of the health implications.

"Willy" did a good job of selling our seminar, though he grumbled that some people who should have bought tickets because they "owed" him didn't buy. Still, he produced a nearly full house in a fairly large theater in Oakland, California. Three-quarters of the way through our second evening, people started leaving the theater. We were warned, and so was "Willy," that the night was not auspicious because of an Oakland Raiders play-off game. When people began to file out to go watch the game "Willy" went bonkers. He hurried up to the stage while Mary was talking and angrily hissed, "What the hell is the matter with you people? You're losing your whole audience. Goddamn it, do something." All told, about 15 percent of the participants left. "Willy's" veins were bulging in his forehead and he was purple in the face.

We calmed him with the soothing words, "It's all right. We knew this was a play-off night; we're thrilled that so many people have stayed." He finally calmed down some but still muttered angrily under his breath. What made his outburst even more pointless was that he had done a good job for the chamber. They got their money, he got his, and the people who stayed really liked the seminar. It was our only encounter with "Willy." A few months later we heard that he'd died of a heart attack. To modify overkill stress, ask yourself if all the anger and powerful response generated by Sabertooth is worth alienating loved ones, colleagues, and bosses or even dying over. That's the question to keep in mind when trying to pacify your Sabertooth.

Because of its volatile nature, Sabertooth comes on quickly. You develop a case of "foot in mouth" disease. It's easy to say things you regret and wouldn't have said at all had you thought them out. Feelings are hurt, remorse and anguish follow, and the stress fallout sends everyone running for cover. Anger that builds all day at work spills out into home life as well. Family members get the brunt of anger that has been held in check all day. People are relieved to learn how to control Sabertooth so they don't yell at their kids when they come home.

We've counseled many concerned employees whose careers were in jeopardy because of Sabertooth behavior and the conflict it caused. These clients were highly motivated because they recognized, and were often told, that Sabertooth had to be controlled or their job was in jeopardy. For this reason it is usually easier to change Sabertooth behavior than it is to change Pleaser. There's often little or no encouragement from others to stop being nice but lots of support for controlling a hot temper. When they learn to manage Sabertooth they feel better about themselves because they're more in control. Work relationships improve when they accept the new perception that the world need not be a dog-eat-dog-place.

QUICK-REFERENCE STRESS TIPS FOR *SABERTOOTH*

Refer to these stress tips to check Sabertooth before it riles you up. Some of the tips are in the chapter; others come from people who have successfully brought Sabertooth to heel.

• Voice opinions without being antagonistic.

• Give people the benefit of the doubt.

• Negotiate your needs.

• Curb impulsive outbursts.

• Listen before you react.

• Consider other people's needs.

• Don't take your anger on the road.

• Invite feedback from others.

• Admit when you're wrong.

• Let go of grudges.

CHAPTER 7

Worrier

When in Doubt, Worry

How to Recognize *Worrier*

Martin leaves his manager Tom's office in a state of apprehension. Things have become unbearable. He never knows from day to day how Tom is going to react. Sometimes he's pleasant, then he does a Jekyll and Hyde. Today he was so abrupt and irritable that Martin left the office shaken. He fears his job may be in jeopardy. Lately, whenever Tom heads in his direction, Martin immediately wonders what he's done wrong. His heart begins to beat faster, and he gets a sinking feeling waiting for the onslaught. Yet nine times out of ten, Tom passes him by. Rumors of another reorganization preoccupy Martin, and he worries that he will be affected adversely by this change. He sometimes doubts that he can handle the current job, let alone a new one, without a lot of supervision from a boss who seems to be less and less available.

Martin picks up the telephone to call one of his vendors to place an order. As a buyer, he's constantly faced with the pressure to get the best price from vendors. But he must also satisfy his internal customers, who hound him to speed up the buying. He hesitates, then puts the phone back down because he doesn't trust that he has enough pricing information yet to make the right decision. "Maybe I should call engineering again," he thinks, then he remembers how irritated they've become with him for calling so often. But he feels the need to verify the data several times before he can trust their accuracy. "It's not their neck if I make the wrong decision," he says to himself, feeling some irritation of his own. Furthermore, it's not all that easy to make a decision.

Sometimes the purchases are very expensive, and he doesn't feel 100 percent comfortable about spending so much money without all the facts. One of his fears is that there will be mistakes or flaws in the materials, hidden at the moment, that will become apparent when it's too late. As his father always cautioned, "Haste makes waste." It's certainly not that Martin doesn't think enough about these decisions he has to make. In fact, he stays awake at night worrying about them. Martin is tormented by a part of himself that doesn't trust him to run his life. That part is his Worrier.

How *Worrier* Causes Stress

Worrier causes you to live in a state of doubt about your ability to take care of yourself. Your personal history of success is disregarded. Survival is credited to the never-ceasing efforts of this Stress Personality. If you don't worry, you're not being serious; you're being frivolous and careless about the dangers that lurk on the treacherous path of life. Fun, relaxation, joy, and forgetting problems are considered irresponsible. The pressure that results from an uneasy preoccupation with potential danger produces anxiousness, dread, fear, and ambivalence. Worry is also a major cause of insomnia. Lack of sleep leads to being chronically tired, dispirited, and apprehensive. This saps energy and vitality. Many unexplained, debilitating "loss of energy" disorders are on the increase. They are exacerbated by worry. After all, what could be more frightening to Worrier than some disease with no name that doctors admit they don't know how to cure?

Advice to the Job Stressed

"When in Doubt, Worry" deals with incidents that typically set off Worrier stress. The first Advice example, "The Incredible Shrinking Job," covers the issue of job security. In a situation worrisome to anyone, the addition of Worrier fears and anxieties puts a downsized employee in a constant state of nervousness. The new perception that will mollify Worrier is that reorganization can be an opportunity.

Next, conflicting duties and expectations grip a worried support engineer, in "Employee Forced to Compete With Himself." He must decide whether to stay in an untenable position or go to a new job with less stress and less security. The lesson here is how to get out of the clutches of Worrier ambivalence.

The following example, "Foot-Draggers Frustrate Nagging Worrier From Hell," discusses the frustrations of trying to get crucial data from tardy colleagues. As deadlines loom, a financial analyst learns that she can reduce her stress by reinterpreting one of her faults, nagging, as an asset.

THE *WORRIER* STRESS TEST

Read the questions below and place a check (✓) in the appropriate column to the right to indicate your response. Find out how your Worrier beliefs and behaviors increase your stress. Pay attention to the questions you checked "Usually" and "Frequently." These have to be reduced to "Occasionally" or "Seldom" in order to control Worrier.	NEVER	SELDOM	OCCASIONALLY	FREQUENTLY	USUALLY
Do I: 1. Believe worry will prevent me from failing? 2. Plan for everything so I'll be prepared for anything? 3. Worry about things I have no control over? 4. Feel that by worrying I'll be prepared for the worst? 5. Feel that if others don't worry as I do, they're irresponsible? 6. Withdraw from people when I'm worried? 7. Rehash problems without arriving at solutions? 8. Avoid risks because I fear the unknown? 9. Obsess over details? 10. Vacillate about decisions because I'm not sure of myself?					

The last example discusses how "The Stress Carrier" infects a work group with worry fever. He needs to place his Worrier in quarantine to help himself and the group recover from this worry epidemic.

Read the "Dear May and Rene" letters. The replies to these letters will show how you can calm and reassure your Worrier.

STRESSOR  TOPIC

HOW TO MANAGE THE STRESS OF DOWNSIZING

People handle the stress of reorganization and downsizing in different ways. Some regard the change as temporary. They ratchet up their efforts, assuming eventually things will return to normal and their stress will even out. Others feel lost and fail to thrive in these chaotic, uncertain conditions. Still others, those who've been reorganized dozens of times, throw up their hands and go with the flow. Downsizing can also leave people stranded without a clear job description. Or they have to scramble with ingenuity to create a value-added position. The lack of job definition is sure to bring on Worrier fear. This Stress Personality cripples you by draining all your energy with worry and prevents you from finding a safer mooring. In the following case, a downsized former project coordinator fears that she'll be fired if she can't meet the requirements of a nonexistent role.

The Incredible Shrinking Job

Dear Mary and Rene,

I've been reorganized three times this year. Every time I'm reorged into a new position, there are fewer people and my job is less defined. My new manager is vague about my new role. He's either being evasive when I ask him about it or doesn't know himself what it will be. Two years ago I was project coordinator and had fourteen people reporting to me. After the three reorganizations, no one reports to me. I'm in a constant state of nervousness. Without a job description, I don't have a clear understanding of where I'm headed in this organization. If I don't have a clear role, maybe my position will be eliminated. When I don't know what's going on, I get very uncomfortable and feel uneasy. I'm afraid I won't meet the requirements of the job, whatever they're supposed to be, because I'm not sure what they are. If I don't find out soon, I could be redeployed or laid off. At times I worry to the point of becoming immobilized. At work I keep to myself to try to find an answer. I'm exhausted and can't sleep and have been diagnosed with irritable bowel syndrome. I need to know how to get worry under control.

Searching for Job Security

Dear Shrinking Job,

Worrier is the part of you that likes stability, and change is unsettling. Your Worrier will cause you to regard things as worse than they are. Anybody who's been reorganized three times in a year, with a manager who's vague about the job description, would feel stress. The manager seems to be as much at sea as you. If he doesn't know what he's doing himself, he's not going to be much help at this time.

An important new perception that might seem scary to your Worrier but can reduce stress in the long run is that there is no job security anymore. When you accept this fact of life, you can stop focusing on the vague and uncertain future and concentrate on what's happening at the moment. Ask yourself what opportunities are available in this chaotic, uncertain time. Many companies today are urging employees to create and justify their own jobs. Think of yourself as being self-employed. This is a perfect opportunity to create your own role. It will be harder to eliminate your position if you've created a value-added, useful role.

Worrier stressful perceptions that are hampering you are the following:

- If you don't always know what's going on it must be bad.
- Isolating yourself will help you find solutions.
- You'll be fired if you can't meet the requirements of a nonexistent role.

Not fully understanding what's going on does not have to be a handicap. One new perception for Worrier that is as old as the hills is: no news is good news. Sometimes this can mobilize you and free you to go about your business. A clearly defined job description won't guarantee job security anyway. Many people with clearly defined jobs, who are performing heroically, get fired during a downsizing. You seem to think a clear definition will act as a talisman to keep away evil spirits. The fact that your job description is murky need not put you in jeopardy. This preoccupation stops you from moving into action and creating a role. The following stress tips will help you focus attention on how you can improve job security.

Keep your mind focused on establishing your value.

 You need to be imaginative and focused during the chaos of reorganization. It may seem you are starting over, but you never really start from scratch. You bring with you all the accumulated knowledge and experience of your work life. Ask yourself, "How do I mine my knowledge to insure that I add value?" Choose one of your best skills and see how many ways you can apply it during the reorg. New conditions are an opportunity to make yourself invaluable and enhance job security. As long as you remain valuable, you'll have a job. Worry is the last thing you need if you want to create this upbeat frame of mind. These proactive steps will wrench your destiny out of the clutching hands of Worrier.

Talk to your manager.

Get as much information from your manager as possible. Many managers feel that part of the management role is to have all the answers. When they are in the dark themselves they compound the apprehension in subordinates by acting evasive or inaccessible. Let the manager know that it's OK with you for him not to know what's going on yet. You'd rather hear "I don't know" than nothing. The more open you are to hearing "I don't know yet," the more you'll encourage straight talk. If your manager sees that telling you the truth sets off a panic reaction in you, he will soon clam up. Then he will seem evasive. So keep those communication channels open.

Stress Tips Summary

When Shrinking expands her viewpoint, Worrier will have less influence. She can work toward adding value, network with colleagues, and work with her manager to define her role.

TOPIC   SUMMARY

Reorganization as Opportunity

Dear Readers,

One way to reassure Worrier is to realize that reorganizations have predictable phases. In every reorg, there are three recognizable stages that correspond to the stress response itself: resistance, adaptation, and resolution.

Resistance is phase one of reorganization. When speculation becomes fact, disbelief is often the first response. Worrier reactions in this phase include alarm, fear, loss of motivation, and worry. For Worrier, the change represented by a reorg will initially be seen as potentially disastrous. That's why it's important to turn anxiety into excitement. This will open your eyes to opportunities. Good things can come of a reorganization when you start making the best of it right away.

Phase two is adaptation. Change is happening daily. The right hand doesn't know what the left is doing. There is confusion and chaos. Worrier reactions in this phase are directed toward trying to establish some sense of stability. But because you don't know how things are going to shake out, Worrier can paralyze you. You hang on to the resistance phase and don't move into coping mode. What's most helpful here is to know that this is a *stage,* and is to be expected. It too shall pass, and stability will be established.

Next is phase three, resolution. A relative state of order and routine can be expected. At this point Worrier begins to feel comfortable. By now, you have sniffed out the trail and know where you're going. You reach this phase sooner if you're proactive instead of just letting things happen to you.

Remember, there will be blips, deviations, and changes of direction. This is not a static state. Now formal role clarification becomes essential and possible. Worrier will be fairly quiescent during this time. Encourage yourself to experiment and take risks as a necessary ingredient for growth.

When you can recognize these expected phases, you will have more control over Worrier. Reassure this Stress Personality, "Yes, I know things are up in the air; that's how they're supposed to be. Soon they will settle down again." But be aware: Another round of reorg is in the cards, and, eventually, off you'll go again as the cycle begins anew.

For Worrier, change and instability create foreboding and a need to cling to the status quo. This can make it difficult when you need to make changes in your life to further your career. Shell-shock from restructuring and terror of downsizing as you make decisions that have to do with your future is a recipe that is sure to bring on Worrier.

STRESSOR  TOPIC

HOW TO MAKE DECISIONS WHEN IN DOUBT

Making decisions involves taking risks. Since Worrier considers its role is to protect you from disaster, it will scrutinize any potential risk and pronounce it "too risky." Your present position, no matter how bad, is better than the unknown, according to Worrier. However, there is one way Worrier will allow you to consider taking a risk. If you ruminate about the decision constantly, and seek opinions from everyone you can think of, the right answer may emerge. "But," says Worrier, "it may not. And if it does, how can you be sure it's the right answer?" So the decision is made, then unmade repeatedly, and you remain in the deep "stresspool" of ambivalence, as illustrated in the following Advice case.

Employee Forced To Compete With Himself

Dear Mary and Rene,

I'm currently assigned to two organizations that have conflicting charters. I must support both even though one charter could be at odds with the other. My manager wants me to give support to his group but sell my consulting services to the other manager's group I'm supposed to support. I've tried getting direction from my manager as to how to handle these conflicting responsibilities but have been unsuccessful. I recognize that I'm between a rock and a hard place. It's causing anxiety attacks. When I get a phone call from either manager, I hyperventilate and experience rapid heartbeat.

Recently, a job I looked at a couple of years ago has become available. I have reason to believe that if I apply I'll get this job. Although it pays less initially, there is room for advancement, and it's not as stressful. Because I would be the newest person in the group, I'm fearful that I'd be the most vulnerable in a reorg. My current job does offer a high profile in the company, which is good for my career. But it's such a difficult position to be in that too much visibility might be a detriment. I need to make a decision soon before the other opportunity goes away. My family and friends are tired of watching me vacillate about this decision. One day I make a firm resolve one way, and the next day I reverse directions. I seem ready to make a decision, then, like a ball of yarn unraveling, I undo it. How do I make the right decision?

Handcuffed by Indecision

Dear Forced,

From your description, it seems that you can't decide to decide. You're being forced to compete with your Worrier's ambivalence, and so far, you're losing. Worrier will "yes, but" you to death and never let you make a decision. One "yes, but" is, "I'm locked in a no-win vise that is causing me stress, but if I move to another job, I'll be vulnerable to reorganization." Another is, "My current job offers me a high profile in the company, but if I fail it will be visible to everyone."

Your Worrier is operating from the stressful perception that there is a right way to handle this mission impossible. In this job, you are at cross purposes, stuck with conflicting charters. This is sure to arouse your Worrier. Often, decisions get made by default because of Worrier handwringing. They also don't get made for the same reason, and you lose a chance at opportunity because of this Stress Personality's indecision.

Worrier traits that are elevating your stress here include:

- Talking this matter to death with family and friends
- Firm resolve on Monday that dissolves into jelly on Tuesday
- Keeping the decision-making process open-ended

A new perception is that it's safer to make a decision one way or the other, because you can't go in opposite directions at once. This internal tug-of-war is tearing you apart. You have to make up your mind what's most important. Do you want to continue in a high-profile position and reap whatever benefit is possible? Or do you want to bail out to avoid the risk of a public hanging for some spectacular flop? If you decide to stay, your manager is unequivocal about what he wants from you. Can you live with that? You fear the risk inherent in the new because you'd be low on the totem pole, but how secure are you now?

Asking yourself these questions can lead you to your decision, but you've got to shut your Worrier up, temporarily at least. The stress tips to follow provide an understanding of how Worrier hampers decision making and what you can do to change.

STRESS TIPS TAKING ACTION BRIDGES THE DIVIDE

Put limits on the amount of time you take to make a decision.

 It's time to act. Gather information before you decide, but don't overdo it. After you've talked the matter to death, driving family and friends nuts, that's enough. Your decision-making time is limited by the other opportunity, which won't wait forever. Whatever you decide, keep Worrier out of the loop, because this Stress Personality will continue to surface fresh doubts. The tendency to vacillate drags out the process and increases stress. Set a time when you'll decide, and assure Worrier that if things don't work out, you can always change directions. Give the new choice a chance. It takes every bit of confidence you can muster to launch a new career opportunity.

Get these managers together to hash out the problem.

As long as you're on this job, deal with the imme-diate concern first. You've got two managers in conflict over your services. That's their problem as well as yours. Tell the managers of both organizations to decide how they want to divide your time. This forces them to deal with the discongruency. It sounds like these organizations are in competition. This fact will surface when you give them the issue to resolve. Let them lose sleep over it. Share the wealth.

Counter Worrier's qualifying language with decisiveness.

When you realize that your language is full of qualifications, you can be sure it's Worrier talking. Beset by doubt and issuing nervous caveats, Worrier says, "What if I do the wrong thing? I'm never sure what to do, but I have to do something." Counter with, "I'm always sure what to do, and I always do something." Change Worrier's tentative, uncertain language, because it increases fear of the future. Instead, use forceful and reassuring certainties, which will calm you. For instance, remind Worrier that you've been making good decisions all your life or you wouldn't be where you are. You are a successful, competent person. The proof of this is that two managers are competing for you, and a third one is offering a job. What more do you need, a bouquet of flowers?

Stress Tips Summary

When Forced puts these stress tips into action, he will seize the momentum from his Worrier. He will surface the issue by bringing it to the attention of the managers. Next, he will set a time limit on how long to take for the decision, and once he feels more decisive, he will have the confidence to make the decision work out.

TOPIC  SUMMARY

When in Doubt, Stop Worrying

Dear Readers,

To Worrier, decisions once made are irrevocable. No wonder it's so important to avoid a bad one. We could argue that Forced made a poor decision because he's in a job with conflicting mandates. But did he? Consider the choices that were made to get him where he is today. At some point he left a job to take this one. Although his decision looks like it led him down a cul-de-sac of conflicting charters, he's been successful in it for at least two years. Meanwhile, another job he once wanted has reappeared. Two managers are fighting over his services, and a third one is offering him a job. His decision to take the current position resulted not in disaster but in opportunity. How could it have been a bad decision?

There is no way to know ahead of time where a decision will lead. The Worrier way is stressful because of the presumption that somewhere down the path, pitfalls lie waiting to trap the unwary. Visualizing images of doom or catastrophe won't prevent unpleasant things from happening. Life contains both the good and the bad and, as the popular bumper sticker proclaims, "shit happens." The trouble with Worrier is that this Stress Personality creates stress before there is any reason for it. Every decision or choice is blown up into a momentous life crisis.

Sometimes you will make bad decisions. The point is, they are not fatal. You've already made some in the past and have lived through them. No doubt they were painful and you experienced regret. But Worrier can't save you from the pain by trying to insure you never make another one. The stress that hobbles you comes from the worry itself. When you're consumed by fear, doubt, and trepidation over long periods of time, it wears you down. You can't think clearly or assess realistically, which in turn hampers your ability to make sensible decisions. When you put Worrier to rest, you open up all kinds of creative avenues for solving dilemmas.

Once a decision is made, whether it's stay or go, you still have to live with Worrier. Just trying to get your work done under Worrier pressure can affect your self-image and destroy your self-confidence. One way to prevent this is to figure out how to use your Worrier traits to your advantage.

STRESSOR TOPIC

HOW TO TURN WORRY INTO AN ASSET

One of the ways Worrier causes stress is through the domino effect of serialized worry. This process links each potential disaster to the inevitable next one, to still a third, and on down the line until you're flattened and destitute. This same type of analytic thinking can be helpful in planning, provided you temper Worrier's exaggerated fears. You could serialize perceived successes and carefully plan a strategy to achieve them.

Another Worrier trait that can be an advantage is perseverance, which is a positive aspect of persistence. Worrier may be a nervous Nellie but is certainly no shrinking Violet. This quality of hanging on steadfastly is an asset. But when Worrier labels an effective response as a possible detriment, the ordinary stress of making a deadline becomes worse, as in the following Advice example.

Foot-Draggers Frustrate Nagging Worrier From Hell

Dear Mary and Rene,

I'm obsessive about meeting my monthly deadlines. I have to rely on three people for information. Two of them are always late. When they don't deliver the data, my financial reports are delayed. So I have to do everything at the last minute and worry that in my haste to finish, I'll make mistakes. No matter how much I try to prod these two, nothing seems to work. I keep after the foot-draggers because I don't know what else to do, yet I don't want to come across as the nagging worrier from hell.

Toward the end of each month I begin to anticipate another hassle with them. I start worrying day and night, lose sleep thinking about it, get headaches, and feel helpless to control the situation. I worry about all the things that could happen if I don't get the figures on time. I could look bad, the report could be flawed, my manager could get upset with me, I might get a poor review, and on and on. When I finally get this last-minute information I skip lunch, stay late, and come in early to insure the deadline will be met. I shift into high, type like a maniac, turn in the report, go home, and crash and burn. Once again, a disaster is averted. How can I get people to cooperate without worrying and nagging?

Bedeviled by Delinquent Data

Dear Nagging Worrier,

Most of the stress here is coming from your Worrier. You are a successful person coping with a difficult assignment every month and doing it effectively. Yet to this Stress Personality, the problem is totally out of control and your plight verges on disaster. The Worrier alarms you by laying out a scary scenario of serialized worry: If the report is flawed, the manager gets upset and gives you a poor review, and naturally this means you lose your job, home, and family and will end up a bag lady, until you finally lose your Safeway shopping cart. If that interpretation of yourself were true, you would indeed have something to worry about. But none of these things have happened, nor are they likely to.

When you accept Worrier's interpretation, you react to the events as if they had already happened. This excess worry fogs your imagination by totally preoccupying your mind, and you can't think of solutions for anything. There is nothing left in your "thought generator" for figuring out what to do. Worrier impedes the search for new ideas or solutions by continually obsessing on the potential horrific outcomes. You get a double dose of stress. You imagine the worst, believe it, then experience the stress of the thought as if it had really happened. You suffer the same amount of stress as if you had actually gone through that trauma.

Some Worrier stressful perceptions that raise your stress needlessly include the following: You

■ Constantly expect the worst case scenario to unfold so you'll be prepared

■ Feel helpless if you can't get people to cooperate

■ Believe if you turn into a maniac or nagging worrier from hell, you can avert disaster

Expecting the worst-case scenario *is* the worst-case scenario in your case. All it does is needlessly stir up your system with adrenaline, and it doesn't solve anything. Labeling yourself helpless scares your Worrier even more. Now security is no longer in the "good hands of Allstate" but in the shaky hands of someone who is helpless. Ye gods!! But just because you want to take care of yourself doesn't mean you're a maniacal, nagging worrier. In fact, you are handling the Internal Time-keeper behavior of the foot-draggers perfectly. You have to nip like a hound at their heels consistently and relentlessly.

The first stress tip adopts a new perception to help you take a new look at yourself and what you're doing.

STRESS TIPS   NAGGING WORRIER BECOMES A RELENTLESS GO-GETTER

Re-label your behavior to change your attitude.

 Re-frame your self-image from the "nagging worrier from hell who works like a maniac" to "the persistent, relentless go-getter of the financial analyst's office." Persistence is not a negative quality in this affair but a valuable one. For Worrier, persistence is a built-in attribute of obsessiveness. Use it to get the information you need. If the foot-draggers are operating in Internal Timekeeper mode, they'll probably appreciate the reminders. You are already doing what you need to do. Keep it up without all the stress. When you re-label your behavior, it will improve your attitude and demeanor. You no longer have to feel the pressured urgency that comes from "nagging" and can substitute calm, persistent assertiveness.

Do whatever it takes to get the attention of the foot-draggers.

 Action is a good antidote for Worrier. Can you enlist the cooperation of your manager and get him to ring some bells? Sometimes a problem has to be kicked up to a higher level for faster resolution. Consider convening a meeting and discussing this subject with managers, foot-draggers, and anyone else in the loop.

Concentrate on the reality that you've been successful getting the data so that's not a concern. The only problem you're there to solve is *when* you get the data. This helps keep Worrier from blowing the problem into a larger matter than it needs to be.

Say good night to Worrier.

 The middle of the night is not the time to engage in conversation with Worrier. Everything looks worse at night. From Worrier's perspective, you're not doing anything but sleeping anyway, so this is a good time to ruminate about worries. You have to put a stop to that. When Worrier wakes you up, say, "Not now," and agree on a time to discuss concerns the next day. You must keep that appointment with Worrier, because trust is an issue for this Stress Personality. Failure to keep your appointment will stir up Worrier, and your credibility will be trashed. The next day, keep the meeting short and discuss only one or two worries and possible solutions. Do this every time Worrier wakes you to worry.

Stress Tips Summary

When Nagging Worrier becomes a persistent go-getter, she will have followed these stress tips successfully. She can now think of herself in a new, less anxious way. She's doing a good job of solving most of her problems, and any left can be shared and brainstormed with her manager and others.

TOPIC  SUMMARY

Lay Your Worries on the Doorstep

Dear Readers,

At night, you need all the help you can muster to silence Worrier and get a good night's sleep. Pharmaceutical companies have no worry about their future, because one in every five people takes some form of sleeping medication. Stanford University even has a sleep clinic because sleep disorders are so pervasive.

Worrier is the usual bogeyman causing sleep disturbances. When you are relaxed and feeling little stress, it's easier to sleep. Relaxation tapes have proven effective for people who've attended our stress management programs, and so have visualizations.

Here is a simple exercise you and your Worrier can do together in the middle of the night: When Worrier wakes you up and doesn't respond to your promise to discuss worries in the morning, visualize a drawer or box. Make it an ornate and important box or drawer. Imagine placing the worries in one of these containers, and putting it away, somewhere safe. Worry is a ritualized behavior, so Worrier will respond if you make this visualization into a ritual. Practice this exercise regularly and you will control nighttime worry. Sweet dreams.

Now that we've discussed how to stop Worrier from aggravating you, it's time to take a look at how you can prevent this Stress Personality from infecting others. Worrier is hard to handle at work and at home. In many families, a Worrier parent is often kept in the dark about important issues because everyone wants to avoid setting off the worry cycle. At work, colleagues hide in bathrooms or any place that affords a refuge from having to listen to a co-worker consumed by Worrier.

STRESSOR TOPIC

HOW TO CONTAIN WORRY

Worrier switches concerns like a chameleon changes colors. You have a good job that is quite secure, but can you afford a home? You decide you can. Then Worrier jumps in with, "Of course, but you have to stay healthy," and you start worrying about health. Then it switches to job security and says, "If you can keep your job, fine, but what if something happens now that you're in debt up to your eyeballs?" In order to reassure yourself, you use other people as sounding boards. But Worrier overdoes it. As you're talking to them you're passing along an subterranean flow of worry that seeps into their unconscious minds. Instead of feeling better after airing your worries, you still feel anxious, and people catch your sense of foreboding. Now they're infected and pass it to the next Worrier, and a whole group becomes susceptible, as in the following Advice example.

The Stress Carrier

Dear Mary and Rene,

I've been told by co-workers, including the manager, that I'm a stress carrier. I can't deny that, because I'm under a great deal of stress. I'm worried that I've taken on more than I can handle financially by buying a home. Buying cost more than was projected, and financial insecurity is constantly preying on my mind. I have a tendency to talk about this all the time. The people I work with have been nice about listening and giving advice. Despite all the reassurance, nothing seems to ease my worries.

Colleagues have assured me that home values are going up rapidly in this area and that homes are a good investment. But there was a severe hurricane a few years ago that affected property values. Recently, my job performance has suffered because I'm so nervous, jumpy, and unfocused. The other day in a meeting I was impatient and short-tempered over a move we were making from one building to another. I didn't think the move was going well and felt a great urgency to make others see the possible pitfalls.

In one instance, I got on the manager's case in a public setting. Afterwards, she called me into her office and warned me that I was causing stress for everyone. We've always been a tight-knit group who depend on each other. But since that incident, co-workers seem to be avoiding me like the plague. On top of the financial insecurity, now my boss is mad at me and my job could be in jeopardy. How do I stop this worrying and quit being a stress carrier?

Worry Contagion Spreads Through Work Group

Dear Stress Carrier,

It's not you that's the stress carrier; it's your Worrier. Worry is contagious. When you approach people in a panic mode every day over something you perceive as a crisis, they have two choices. One is to give you advice and reassurance to try settling you down. The other is to avoid you. Those prone to Worrier behavior themselves will catch the virus, and they, too, will be anxious. Worry spreads not only from person to person but also from problem to problem. The urgency you feel over your home buying decision infected the group and was applied to the office move. One worry precipitated the other.

Here are some of the Worrier stressful perceptions that make you contagious:

■ You can never get enough advice.

■ If you worry about questionable decisions, you'll do better next time.

■ It's important that others also worry over possible pitfalls.

When you feel a stirring need to set out on another "advice patrol," heed this new perception: Too much advice can overload your Worrier circuits. Asking continually for help is just another way to keep you engaged in the Worrier process. Stop yourself and say, "No, I can trust myself to do the right things." There comes a point at which the surplus advice becomes meaningless and you stop taking any of it in. Then colleagues get irritated when you come back and ask for still more, which they know you'll ignore. When people tell you that property values increased in the area and you made a good choice, believe them. What's the point of not believing, since the advice could make you feel better?

Security lies not in worrying over decisions you've already made, but in making sure those decisions work to your advantage. No amount of worry will prevent hurricanes. They are a fact of life where you live. Prepare yourself for them just as you would for the so-called pitfalls you were warning the group against. Also, read the real estate section of the newspaper, not the just the front page. All media play to Worrier subscribers. Any day of the week, if you run short of worries, the newspapers offer a cornucopia of disasters, holocausts, and tragedies happening to people you don't know and never will. Reading the real estate section will keep you informed and reassured. The following stress tips will sedate your Worrier without requiring quarantine.

Refocus Worrier to lower your stress.

Concentrate on enjoying your home. You've got a piece of the American dream and have turned it into a nightmare. Your jumpy nervousness is a symptom of Worrier's edgy, frightened view of your present circumstances. Buying real estate is a common stressor, but the worry is usually centered around the buying transaction itself. You're past that high-stress threshold, so it's time to recover. Move to the homeowner phase. Ease Worrier's fear of falling real estate prices by making sure the property stays valuable. Fix it up. Plant a tree or two. Every time Worrier trots out the "financial ruin" routine, go do something constructive. Keep Worrier's handwringing occupied with home improvement.

Refrain from taking on other people's worries or insisting they join in yours.

Don't spread worry contagion. Keep your worrying to yourself. Since worry is contagious, you can catch it or spread it. Any good Worrier wants everyone in on the action. Worrier believes others who don't worry along with you are un-caring, unconcerned, unloving, or unreliable. Instead of trying to pull others into your worry web, ask for the kind of feedback that can be most helpful: facts, actions, and options you can act on. Also, ask for feedback when others notice you going into your doomsday predictions. Tell them you're trying to change. Awareness itself can help you reverse directions.

Stress Tips Summary

The stress tips for Stress Carrier are focused on containing the Worrier bandwidth. These new approaches will redirect his attention. He'll trust his decisions and refrain from ask-ing for needless advice. Instead of spreading stress he can work on a new treatment for his Worrier.

TOPIC  SUMMARY

Worry Fever Contained

Dear Readers,

Financial worries are an outgrowth of job insecurity which has been much in the news. Horror stories of corporate restructuring that costs the jobs of thousands are fodder for Worrier. Every new story of job losses reinforces Worrier's fear that you are "just two paychecks from the street." Unfortunately, many people are, but Worrier makes no distinction between those who are and those who aren't.

An effective way to contain Worrier is to train yourself to decide when you will worry about something and not let Worrier call the worry meeting. This puts things in your hands and calms Worrier, because now this Stress Personality knows somebody is in charge here. Often, worries that seem ominous at night tend to fade into normal non-emergency concerns in the daylight. Just as people are often advised to leave their work worries at work, you need to leave your home worries at home and your night worries for day.

POSTSCRIPT

Security Means Trusting Yourself

Dear Readers,

Job security is a loaded issue for everyone these days. In our research we've seen an increase of Worrier response around this topic. People speak of headcount reductions happening almost daily. Frequent reorganizations are experienced as a perverse game of musical chairs. When the music stops there are fewer chairs than people, and out go those left standing.

Any shift of circumstances that affects those already living on the financial edge is a shock. Just when you have a sense of economic security, you're reorganized and your spouse is reengineered out of a job. Without a crystal ball, it's hard to foretell the future. If you wait until you're guaranteed job security to live your life, you'll never take the chances that enrich life. So what is job security? Can you live without it or create it in a different form?

Job Security—Always Work for Yourself

Actually, working for yourself means not a change in employment but a change in perspective. You can shift from getting your security from a job to getting it from yourself. A new perception for this is: No matter whom you work for, you are ultimately working for yourself. This perception is the best form of security there is. It means trust yourself. Worrier sabotages self-trust by instilling doubt. While doubt is normal and at times sensible, you cannot live in a constant state of uncertainty, dread, and fear.

To prove to your Worrier how trustworthy you really are, do the following: Take out a piece of paper and assess the decisions you've made in your life that got you to where you are now. Think of a time when you were really in a jam. Perhaps you'd been laid off, or you moved to a new area without already having a job. Then note how you solved this crisis, especially any of the excellent choices, ideas, or actions that helped lead you out of the wilderness. The same person that handled that mess in the past is still available to you. That person who looked for a job and got one is your real employer. And you can assure your Worrier that's the person to trust to take care of you.

When a Loss Is a Win

We recently heard an interesting contrast to the usual fear of layoffs. A young woman told our stress management class, "Oh, I love to get laid off." Naturally, everyone looked a bit startled. She went on to explain that the best advances in her career had come from being laid off. The first time it happened, the company had downsized too severely and suffered from an acute case of corporate anorexia. She received a nice severance package and a few weeks later was hired back by her desperate former employer, who discovered that her skills were not replaceable. The second time it happened, she used the opportunity to travel to Southeast Asia for a while.

She came back refreshed and full of adventure and found a much better job. Now it had happened again. Once more, she received a fat severance package, and she decided after a talk with her manager to take it and go back to school—something she'd wanted to do for years. She was assured that with her new skills, she would command a higher salary. "When lay-offs are in the offing," she exclaimed, "I perk right up."

Penetrating the *Worrier* Wall

We've seen whole groups get sucked in by a determined Worrier who won't let any sound suggestions penetrate their worry barrier. The determined Worrier presents a seemingly insoluble problem to the group and asks for help. People jump in enthusiastically with proposed solutions. But the ideas bounce off the worried person like bullets off a bulletproof vest. One idea after another is presented, only to be met with, "Oh, I've tried that and it didn't work," or, "Yes, but you don't understand; you see, I can't, and it's because . . . ," and on goes the dirge until one by one the other participants fall silent. Only the most dogged Strivers continue to offer surefire solutions, but eventually even they throw up their hands in frustration. And then a kind of Worrier pall sets in and the room goes silent, until we ask the question, "Are we feeling helpless yet?" There is a relieved chorus of yes from all. Our response is, "That's what it feels like both internally and externally to struggle with Worrier."

The object of the worry process is to fend off help by making sure none gets through. While engaging the group in this exercise may seem futile and discouraging, especially for the "stuck" Worrier, it almost always has a positive effect. Later in the day the person gets a breakthrough, allows ideas in, and solves the puzzle. The light bulb comes on because the Worrier process has been identified and the inference that there is no answer has been challenged.

Many people mistake worrying for planning, but worrying is not action oriented, whereas planning is. That's why almost every tip has some advice to move to action. Moving to action involves planning. Unlike Internal Timekeeper, where action takes the place of planning and increases stress, planning for Worrier is like a road map of action. Always ask yourself,

"What are two proactive steps I can take instead of worrying?" It's the most effective way to break the bonds of Worrier. When in doubt, instead of worrying, follow the stress tips and the quick-reference guide for Worrier.

QUICK-REFERENCE STRESS TIPS FOR *WORRIER*

To keep Worrier from causing you sleepless nights and worried days, refer to these quick stress tips:

- When in doubt, be proactive.
- Concentrate on what is happening, not what could happen.
- Leave work worries at the office and home worries at home.
- Trust yourself.
- Limit your time for worry, then shut it off.
- Make decisions based on facts you have at the time.
- Limit what you're going to worry about.
- Recognize, accept, and build on your successes.
- View change as challenge and excitement.
- Compartmentalize worry to keep from being overwhelmed.

Inner Con Artist

Always Put Off Till Tomorrow . . .

How to Recognize Your *Inner Con Artist*

Dennis sits in his office staring at the wall. He glances at his watch. "Almost time to go home," he tells himself, feeling a sense of relief. Another fruitless day is about over. He steps out his door and looks down the hall to his manager's office. The lights are off, and Dennis realizes he's gone. "Hell, I might as well leave early," he thinks. "There's no point in starting anything this late in the day anyway, and I've still got plenty of light left for a few rounds of golf."

As he furtively maneuvers his way to the parking lot, Dennis feels some guilt and disgust at himself. Lately he's been finding ways to duck out of work. It's not like him, but he's frustrated and unhappy. The work is no longer emotionally satisfying, and he doesn't enjoy it anymore. Part of the reason he's losing interest is that his job is boring and he doesn't feel challenged.

To Dennis, the root cause of his discontent is that he has to work at something he doesn't like. He feels cheated that he hasn't been able to earn a living in a job that is related to something he loves doing. This sense of apathy is new to Dennis. In every other position he's had, including this one at the start, if he had any fault it was that he worked too hard. Though he's certainly not overtaxing himself now, he always feels drained of energy. In the last six months he's lost interest in exercising and has gained twenty pounds. Recently an old fantasy of going into wine making has been encroaching on his thoughts.

Procrastination has crept in at work and at home. His wife has a mile-long "Honey Do" list and a short fuse. She has made it clear to him that she's sick of him promising to do chores that he never gets to. At work he's feeling pressured by his manager to do "whatever it takes" to finish the project he's been working on. But Dennis has developed a "Who cares?" attitude. "Why bust my buns at a job I don't like and nobody appreciates anyway," he rationalizes. The whiff of telltale smoke that hovers around Dennis is a warning sign of burnout. And his Inner Con Artist has taken over his life.

How *Inner Con Artist* Causes Stress

This Stress Personality abhors doing anything that requires discipline and persistence. The easy way out becomes habitual. You develop a pattern of starting things then dropping them because they require too much effort. Then you criticize yourself for not getting anywhere. "There you go again. What's the matter with you? Don't you have any willpower?" you scold yourself. Disgusted for not living up to your own promises, you feel guilt and defeat. To get away from these unpleasant feelings, you call in Inner Con Artist to help you forget them through denial, which produces an "eraser effect": Unpleasant events and self-defeating actions are wiped clean from your memory. The headache from yesterday's hangover is forgotten. When cocktail hour comes around you find yourself with a drink in your hand. In this way, Inner Con Artist exacerbates addictions and self-destructive behavior.

Advice to the Job Stressed

This chapter highlights stress caused by Inner Con Artist in its varied forms. The first letter, "The Night of the Living Dead Syndrome," discusses job dissatisfaction and the boredom that results. Inner Con Artist behavior as a symptom of burnout is described, and suggestions for infusing new energy into a dying career are offered.

Winning the procrastination battle is the subject of "Addicted Procrastinator Seduced by Games." For those struggling with Inner Con Artist, procrastination is a primary detour on the road to success. Advice for the procrastinator includes how to work around Con Artist and get on with it.

For busy people, staying healthy is enough of a challenge without adding the subversion of Inner Con Artist. In the "Inner Con Artist Health Plan," a new manager increases the stress of her job by jeopardizing her health. Stress tips focus on how to maintain accountability to herself and her health plan.

Drastic, stressful life changes that are too much to handle are the subject of "The TV, a Twelve-Pack, and Me." It describes how an attempt to numb painful losses results in self-defeating behavior. How to face up to change in a healthy way is the focus of the advice.

THE *INNER CON ARTIST* STRESS TEST

Read the questions below and place a check (✓) in the appropriate column to the right to indicate your response. Find out how your Inner Con Artist beliefs and behaviors increase your stress. Pay attention to the questions you checked "Usually" and "Frequently." These have to be reduced to "Occasionally" or "Seldom" in order to control Inner Con Artist.	NEVER	SELDOM	OCCASIONALLY	FREQUENTLY	USUALLY
Do I: 1. Procrastinate when facing a difficult assignment? 2. Reward myself with things I should abstain from when I feel deprived? 3. Avoid dealing with tough personal problems? 4. Grab for immediate gratification to relieve job stress? 5. Go on shopping binges when I feel overwhelmed at work? 6. Believe that if I ignore problems they'll go away? 7. Consider self-discipline a form of punishment? 8. Believe that if I get angry about my bad habits I'll change them? 9. Give up or avoid exercise when under stress? 10. Make promises to myself that I don't keep?					

Read the "Dear Mary and Rene" letters. The replies to these letters will offer tips on how to control Con Artist.

STRESSOR  TOPIC

HOW TO STOP HATING YOUR JOB

Inner Con Artist robs you of motivation. You lose enthusiasm and interest in your work. Boredom follows, and now you drag yourself to a boring job day after day. An emptiness caused by a lack of satisfaction opens you to the ministrations of Inner Con Artist. If you regard your work as thankless and uninteresting, you have to obtain fulfillment from some other source. Since you've defined the job as thankless, there's no way to get enjoyment from it, so you turn to Inner Con Artist and begin the slide into nonproductive behavior. As a reward for suffering through a boring job, this Stress Personality treats you with milk and cookies. "Forget the diet. It hurts to exercise, and besides, it's raining," says Con Artist. The best-laid resolutions are undermined. Listlessness sets in, and you walk around in a mechanical trance state, as in the following case.

The Night of the Living Dead Syndrome

Dear Mary and Rene,

I'm beginning to hate my job. My current position is in a high-tension atmosphere. However, coping with irate customers has become less stressful than dealing with upper management, who would rather thumb employees than talk with them. My manager is a control freak who treats us like serfs. Our initiative is stifled because we have to run every idea by him. He disapproves of most but co-opts the ones he likes for himself. I waste time goofing off because I can't do anything my manager will approve of. After five years, I've lost any desire to move upward in the company. For a long time I was disgusted with colleagues who complained or passed the buck. Now I find myself doing the same things I disliked in others. My productivity has decreased to the bare minimum. I'm prone to procrastinate, and my mind wanders. I've pretty much given up on this job. My family complains that I'm withdrawn, and I notice I'm drinking and smoking more. I wander around the office like a zombie from the movie Night of the Living Dead. I just can't stand this any more. How can I get remotivated so I enjoy the job like I used to?

Liven Up a Lifeless Career

Dear Zombie,

You will not raise yourself from the living dead by goofing off with Inner Con Artist. If you have a boring job, it's even more important to find some way to invest enthusiasm and energy into it. Of course, you know there is always the option to quit. But since you didn't mention it, that's not an option you've chosen to take. An Inner Con Artist stressful perception is that you're bored because of the job. A new perception could be that you're bored because you're bringing Inner Con Artist to work with you. This Stress Personality cons you into believing that "goofing off" is a reward for having to endure this hateful job. But fooling around will not bring job satisfaction. Some stressful perceptions of Inner Con Artist that are influencing you include the following:

- If your manager stifles your initiative, you have the right to goof off.
- Because a job is boring, drinking and smoking more are justifiable compensations.
- You can enjoy a job you've given up on.

The reason *Night of Living Dead* is such a vivid metaphor for your problem is that when you've given up on a job you're dead to it. You walk around with stale, zombie-like energy, and every day you go to work and create the conditions you hate. Goofing off and not taking yourself seriously are sure ways to bore yourself to death.

Because your manager doesn't listen to your ideas is no reason for not having any. Your boredom is caused in part by stifling your own creativity and ambition. Taking active steps and resuming initiative are for your benefit, not just your manager's. To inject some new life into your career, read the following stress tips.

STRESS TIPS   REINVIGORATED BY AN ATTITUDE TRANSPLANT

~~~~~~

Always question the Inner Con Artist cause-and-effect cycle.

 Challenge Con Artist excuses that condone your unproductive behavior. When Inner Con Artist suggests that you're forced by circumstances beyond your control to be self-indulgent, counter with a new perception: "I determine what I do and why I do it, and I'll take responsibility." Responsibility must become one of your core values to counter Inner Con Artist's distaste for it. Con Artist "makes up" cause and effect to condone your actions by providing an excuse. You can dismiss your actions because there is a good reason for them, such as you're goofing off because you're bored. Once the excuse is provided, you can continue the behavior. Give Inner Con Artist an ultimatum: "Either I stay on the job and reinvest my energy or I find a new job." What is not acceptable is to stay on the job and goof around.

Examine the situation you're in and decide whether to stay in or get out.

 Reexamine the current job to see if there is a way to infuse it with some excitement. Review the aspects you liked about it when you started. If they are no longer tenable, look for those qualities elsewhere. In many cases Inner Con Artist interludes are situational. It's common for people to change jobs and experience a complete turnaround in attitude and motivation. Look for alternatives. It's hard to make a decision about your future when you're feeling apathetic. Zombie-like energy is not conducive to sparking the ingenuity needed to get you out of this morgue. Inner Con Artist will lull you into a self-defeating lethargy. Rouse yourself by taking active steps to change your job.

Stop rebelling against the control-freak manager and flood him with ideas.

 Be proactive and take the initiative with your manager. Get in his face all the time with ideas. Show him how enthusiastic and creative you are. If your ideas are ripped off or turned down, come back with more. As you do this, it'll be harder for him to keep you under his thumb. He has to loosen up in order to handle your assertiveness. When he requires you to "run every idea by him," do it. Run a truckload of items by him until he's up to his ears in ideas. He will eventually leave you alone in self-defense. After all, he also has others to control, which takes time and energy. A side benefit is that you move out of Inner Con Artist and into productive behavior. A controlling or authoritarian management style will provoke Inner Con Artist. You're better off to confront the manager's controlling behavior and do something about it.

Stress Tips Summary

Zombie will come to life when he puts these stress tips into action. Instead of rebelling against his manager, he can take proactive steps. Rebellion comes from feeling ineffective or weak, like a teenager acting out against an authoritarian parent. When he takes responsibility for doing something about his boring, stifling job, he'll be open to finding new challenges.

TOPIC   SUMMARY

Responsibility—A Personal Value

Dear Readers,

Some people go into Inner Con Artist because they choose to stay in boring, dead-end jobs and manifest the *Night of the Living Dead* syndrome.

They quit working but show up every day. Or they may try to coast to retirement by bringing their bodies to work but leaving their minds at home. "Impending retirement" can be as long as five years.

Other people exhibit Inner Con Artist behavior because they compromise themselves and take jobs they feel overqualified for. For instance, many HMO physicians display Inner Con Artist behavior after a failure to make a go of private fee-for-service practice. To many, it's a comedown to go to work for a medical "factory." The compensation for taking a job that's less than they hope for is to give less back. Inner Con Artist takes over. They're chronically late, shuffle patients off to colleagues, always ask others to cover for them on holidays, and generally don't pull their weight.

Many normally ambitious people have lapsed into bored and unproductive work habits. They don't like it and are puzzled because they know they're acting irresponsibly. It's a major insight to realize that Inner Con Artist is implicated. Once they see this as a part of themselves, a pattern they engage in, choice is introduced. They can either decide to totally invest themselves in the job or leave and take their chances.

When you dislike your work it's understandable to put off work you don't like. But even those who do enjoy their jobs suffer from the stressful practice of procrastination.

STRESSOR TOPIC

WINNING THE PROCRASTINATION BATTLE

Procrastination is the bane of those caught in Inner Con Artist. Although they may revile themselves for it, employees who feel unsure of themselves or overwhelmed can fall into the habit. Looming large on the horizon is a task you have to take on but instead put off, offering a variety of feeble excuses. Day after day passes and you can't seem to get started. The distress mounts as you think about it all the time. Now the task seems insurmountable because you can't get off the dime and get moving. What could have been an interesting challenge turns into an ordeal.

In the following Advice example, a program manager bogs down because she has to perform a feat for which she doesn't feel qualified. Procrastination sets its hook in her, and instead of getting on with it, she treats herself to ice cream and shopping sprees.

Addicted Procrastinator Seduced by Games

Dear Mary and Rene,

As a program manager I'm required to write a materials strategy for each new product program I manage. However, I have never written one. No one in my department has ever written one, including my manager, so I will be the first to attempt this feat. Because I don't know what I'm doing, but have to do it in a hurry, I've tried to get help. I consulted with counterparts in another organization by sending out an SOS over e-mail. Some responses came back, but they seemed too complicated to comprehend. I don't have the time to figure them out. So instead of getting into the material I drift off into fantasies about escaping my job.

When I get frustrated or anxious about not knowing what to do, I procrastinate even more. Even though I've forbidden myself to play computer games at work, I get seduced by the lure of Tetris. I'm afraid I'm addicted. I have pangs of conscience because I'm getting paid but not working. The more time pressure I feel to get going and pro-duce, the more I'm tempted to go on shopping sprees and buy stuff I don't need. I have nervous habits like chewing my nails and playing with my hair. I also gorge myself on ice cream, and my behavior seems beyond my control. How do I stop procrastinating and get into the project?

It's Time to Jilt *Inner Con Artist*

Dear Procrastinator,

Tetris is not the lover who has seduced you, it's Inner Con Artist. Though alluring, the relationship between you and this Stress Personality is self-defeating. It's time for a separation. A way to start is to look at the underlying cause of your need to escape into Con Artist. You may have unrealistic expectations that you can perform a task nobody knows how to do, and do it in a short time frame. Procrastination could be Con Artist's way of suggesting that you need to take another look at the expectations driving this project—both yours and your manager's.

Here are some of the stressful perceptions that indicate you're under the influence of Inner Con Artist:

- Playing computer games when under the gun will reduce stress
- Inner Con Artist likes to rationalize behavior that is forbidden
- Procrastination will postpone frustration and anxiety

There are many reasons Inner Con Artist believes in procrastination. One is that if you're faced with a difficult or distasteful task and put it off, there's an outside chance you won't have to do it. Another is that it's always better to do something fun than to perform a necessary chore, especially if the choice is between an unpleasant duty and an alluring addiction. Procrastination only prolongs frustration and anxiety. The truth is, you can't really put tasks "out of sight, out of mind," because at some level they are always on your mind and will stress you.

You are not alone in your addiction to computer games. This is a stressor for many people. They admit their conscience bothers them for wasting their time and the company's money. This doesn't feel good. You can't forbid Inner Con Artist to stop seducing you with diversions, so don't get into a direct battle with this part of yourself. The following stress tips will help you curb Inner Con Artist's insatiable appetite.

STRESS TIPS   HOW TO CHANGE THE RULES OF THE GAME

Avoid a battle of the wills with Inner Con Artist.

 Focus on achieving what you want to accomplish rather than fighting with your Inner Con Artist. Turn your full attention to figuring out how to write the strategic plan. After all, it could be fun and exciting to be the first to do the impossible. You can't throw Con Artist out the door, because this part of you has survival value, and it's better to accept that fact than deny it. Con Artist would argue that instead of feeling bad because you can't figure out how to do this task, it's better to play games, eat ice cream, and go on shopping sprees. These are fun distractions but lead you away from your objective. The best way to curb this Stress Personality is to make energetic progress toward your goal.

Deal with the unrealistic expectations of yourself and others.

 Work out a sensible schedule that includes the reality that this task has never been done before. Give yourself some leeway, and don't agree to impossible demands. Just because someone has set an arbitrary time frame on a job that nobody knows how to do doesn't mean you have to buy into it. It's typical in companies today to give people an assignment that's never been done and then expect that they do it immediately if not sooner. When you agree to the time schedule and the pressure that goes with it, you get overwhelmed and realize that it's impossible. That's when you invite Inner Con Artist in for ice cream, TV, and *Tetris*. A new perception to help you is that anything you can deliver in the constricted time allowed is better than nothing.

Set a limited initial goal and make time to accomplish it.

 The new perception that accomplishing something is better than nothing will allow you to set a limited goal you can initially reach. Accept what-ever you complete in the time you've given yourself, put it away, and move to something else. Pick it up again the next day and do the same, until you begin to see chunks of progress begin piling up. Soon you'll have more done than not, and you're on your way. Accomplish one modest goal a day and you'll vanquish procrastination. You'll feel good about yourself and feel encouraged to set another modest goal. Achieve that, and you've put a synergistic effect into motion. Once you start achieving results, you won't be as tempted to invite Inner Con Artist to play.

Stress Tips Summary

All these stress tips will help Procrastinator to get up and get moving. She now knows it's pointless to get into a power struggle with Inner Con Artist. When she negotiates a realistic time schedule with her manager, she won't feel as pressured and hence vulnerable to Con Artist escape tactics.

TOPIC   SUMMARY

Don't Put Off Until Tomorrow . . .

Dear Readers,

Self-discipline is necessary to conquer procrastination. To pursue accomplishment requires that you make decisions in your life. Sometimes it's difficult to motivate yourself or dredge up the needed energy to strike off on a new pursuit. Procrastination becomes the choice if you're afraid of being overwhelmed with too much to do and have no time for yourself. Putting things off gives you added time and feeds the hope that the conditions will change and you won't have to do the task. Procrastinators make the point, which is sometimes valid, that it's better to put off decisions or work. Decisions sometimes make themselves, and work may turn out to be unnecessary. This premise is not advisable for those mired in procrastination. Because not acting, rather than acting, is this Stress Personality's predilection.

If we were talking about Internal Timekeeper, it would be a different story with a different recommendation. "Slow down and think before you act," would be the advice, because this Stress Personality has a tendency to jump too quickly to action. This causes wasted effort and the need to undo what has been too quickly started. But this is not the case for Inner Con Artist. Here the advice is, "Get on with it. It's better to do something than nothing." Decisions do bring on responsibility, because once you've decided on a course of action, there will inevitably be work to follow. But make them anyway and get started. When you know you're acting in cahoots with Inner Con Artist, always look to see what action steps you can take. Pay attention to your progress and congratulate yourself for accomplishing important goals. This feeling of pride and self-satisfaction will bring you pleasure without using this inner temptress. Your new motto is: Do it today and there's less work tomorrow.

Procrastination affects every area of your life that requires discipline and persistence. Damage to your career is one effect, but even more serious is when procrastination becomes a health hazard.

STRESSOR TOPIC

HOW TO STAY HEALTHY IN A HIGH-STRESS JOB

One of the negative side effects of too much stress at work is neglect of good health. Busy people working long hours too often give up exercise and subsist on junk food. Even those who have serious health concerns self-destruct when it comes to the persistence and commitment it takes to maintain a health plan. People who have been on medical leave come back to work and sabotage their own progress.

In the next letter, although anguished over her unwillingness to do what it takes to follow her plan, a new manager is unable to put her health first and take care of herself.

The Inner Con Artist Health Plan

Dear Mary and Rene,

I've been promoted to a management position with a large staff and heavy responsibilities. Since I am a new manager, it's important I do well, and I'm afraid that my poor health will keep me from achieving my goals. I'm having great difficulty maintaining a health plan prescribed by the doctor after a serious illness. I've pretty much dropped my low-cholesterol diet; I'm not making needed appointments with the doctor, nor am I taking the medicine as I should. I'm not exercising even though it's convenient, and have gained a lot of weight. I know I should stay away from chocolate bars and other desserts, but it seems like I virtually inhale them. I feel guilty because I'm jeopardizing my health. As the sole breadwinner of my family, if I get sick my family is also in jeopardy. My continued weight gain is undoubtedly raising my cholesterol and my blood pressure, both hereditary conditions. I don't understand why I'm doing this, because a part of me knows better. I'm constantly conning myself by thinking, "Just this one time won't matter." I use excuses to avoid making medical appointments and facing possible bad news. All I think of is short-term gratification. How do I stay on a health plan?

Good Health Is the Best Medicine

Dear Health Planner,

Which health plan are you referring to? Your doctor's or Inner Con Artist's? Right now you are following the latter. The first principle of this Stress Personality's plan is to avoid anything unpleasant such as following your doctor's diet. Your fear of bad news is getting you further away from your desired goal of a sensible health plan. Here are some Inner Con Artist stressful perceptions keeping you from following doctor's orders:

- No news is at least not bad news.
- Just this one time won't matter.
- Self-discipline is punishment.

Your Con Artist doesn't have the needed characteristics to keep you on a health plan. This Stress Personality detests routine, which is necessary especially when regular medication is called for. Self-discipline smacks of "duty" to Con Artist, and duty means doing things you don't want to in order to oblige someone else. This is not the case here. The duty you have is to yourself and family. Forget trying to extract promises from this part of yourself and seize control from this indifferent medical manager.

It's much harder to go to the doctor when you know you are going to be confronted with the results of your inattention to doctor's orders. A medical exam is results oriented and objective. Facts, to Con Artist, are an inconvenience, but they are absolutely necessary if you are to stay healthy. The following stress tips can help you stay on a healthy health plan.

STRESS TIPS   TAKE CONTROL OF YOUR HEALTH

Be accountable to yourself for your health.

View the doctor as an assistant, not an adversary, in helping you carry out *your* plan. It's not your doctor's health plan, it's yours. As long as this health plan is "your doctor's, and he is forcing it on you," Con Artist has the perfect "adult" to rebel against. Inner Con Artist has an impulsive, reckless, and rebellious nature. Once you set up a straw man, you've invited Inner Con Artist to act out. Make the health plan your own by re-labeling it *my* health plan. Now the struggle is out in the open between you and yourself. When you do this, it will flush the Con Artist behavior into consciousness where you can deal with it directly.

Establish a routine.

Establish a routine for taking medication instead of relying on your memory. Set a time that is designated medication time. If you decide it's always 10 A.M., the clock, rather than Inner Con Artist, becomes your health helper. Inner Con Artist causes you to forget unpleasant duties, a form of denial. It's an "out of sight out of mind" version of reality. Routine provides structure and will strengthen your memory. Regular routine helps establish discipline and is an aid to your goal of a healthy life. With this Stress Personality as your medical aide you'll need all the help you can get.

Interrupt the impulse-denial process.

Recognize the fact that you're being influenced by the Inner Con Artist impulse-denial deception. Inner Con Artist is right when it tells you, "Just this one time won't matter," if indeed it is only one time. But it isn't. Inner Con Artist uses its selective memory to cause you to forget what you don't want to remember, such as the fact that you've already indulged ten times this week. This Con Artist "eraser effect" makes it impossible to accurately tally how many digressions you've already made. Of course, one chocolate bar every once in a while might not be harmful. But one bar a day, seven days a week, is thirty bars a month. Multiply that by twelve months and figure out how many pounds of chocolate you eat in a year. Whenever you're tempted, substitute a new jingle: "Just this one time does matter."

Stress Tips Summary

When Health Planner takes over her health plan instead of letting it be her doctor's responsibility, she will be motivated to bring Inner Con Artist into line. When she confronts her denial and establishes a routine it will help her stay the course.

TOPIC SUMMARY

Good Health Is Not Up for Grabs

Dear Readers,

Working in a high-stress environment means it's particularly crucial that you stay healthy. For someone like Health Planner, no news is bad news. When there is a family history of high cholesterol and hypertension, it's doubly important to stay informed. Elevated stress increases the body's production of cholesterol. Add a cholesterol-rich diet, and the chances of heart disease are increased. Hypertension is also made worse by long-term high stress levels. Inner Con Artist is not interested in health, so don't count on this Stress Personality to keep you healthy.

In a high-stress job, it's risky to conclude you don't have time or energy to both get ahead and stay in good shape. The stressful perception is that you have to choose between the two. But you cannot really get ahead without the stamina necessary to flourish in the high-stress environment. Many of our workshop participants complain that they don't have a time or place to exercise. Yet there are always others running on the streets or even doing push-ups in their offices. And many corporations provide fitness facilities for their employees. Although pushing your way through Con Artist excuses can be exhausting, once you get started you'll be on the spiral of good health.

To do this requires close attention to your Inner Con Artist and the will to resist its temptations. Failure results in a spiral of self-defeating behavior that can wreck your life. The next Advice example shows how positive change can come from squarely confronting serious life setbacks.

STRESSOR TOPIC

HOW TO CHANGE SELF-DEFEATING BEHAVIOR

Self-defeating behavior comes in many guises. In the case of Inner Con Artist, procrastination has been mentioned as one example. For Striver it's the tenacious insistence on doing things "my way" which results in having to do everything yourself and wears you out. For Internal Timekeeper it's lack of planning, which causes disorganization. Another form of Inner

Con Artist revolves around denial and obliterating painful stressors through overindulgence. In the following case, we look at self-defeating behavior caused by resistance to change. A man battered by a series of losses avoids facing drastic life upheavals by burying his sorrows in his cups.

The TV, a Twelve-Pack, and Me

Dear Mary and Rene,

Within the past year I lost my job, a friend died in an automobile acci-dent, I got divorced, I moved to another state away from my kids, and I recently started a new job. What's really stressing me now is the new job. It's a marketing position at a large company, whereas before I was strictly in programming. I'd been used to working by myself and just doing what I was trained to do. Now I have to interface with cus-tomers, write and present tutorials, and give technical presentations. My previous job was at a small company where everyone had expertise in their own area. On this one I have to conquer the horror of multi-tasking. I can't seem to get anything done and don't act professional-ly when there are important things to accomplish. I feel unworthy, then procrastinate and give up. I'm constantly irritated that I can't conquer my bad habits of drinking, smoking, and going to bars or staying home with the TV and a twelve-pack. I'm always jittery and feel depressed, bored, unsettled, and guilty for not changing. I've also been withdrawing a lot, I don't eat, and I say to myself, "What's wrong with me?" My question is, why can't I change self-defeating behavior?

You Can't Drown Your Sorrows

Dear Twelve-Pack,

While Inner Con Artist is a good drinking buddy, it's not the best partner to help you through the stress of change. You've gone through big changes in a short time both at home and at work. Any one of these stresses by itself is a lot to deal with. But with all these losses within a year, you're lucky you haven't gotten sick. Inner Con Artist is helping you stay in denial under the faulty perception that this self-defeating behavior is protecting you from feeling the full impact of this turmoil. But obviously it's no longer working given the stress symptoms you're reporting. You're being affected by the following Inner Con Artist stressful perceptions:

- You will change if you feel guilty enough.
- If you ignore pain and unpleasant feelings you won't feel stressed.
- If you're angry at yourself over bad habits, you'll drop them.

When you deny, ignore, or minimize serious issues because you don't want to deal with them, it's an attempt to cope with stress. You've grossly underestimated the impact of losing your friend, marriage, home, and children. It's common for people to deal with loss through Inner Con Artist in an attempt to minimize the pain.

Booze dulls the senses, which helps some, but it's only temporary. Sooner or later you will have to deal with these losses by experiencing the emotional impact. If your company has an employee assistance program, this would be a good support for you during this time of change. You could use some ongoing help.

One source of the guilt you mention could be remorse at letting your Con Artist undermine your normal productive and reliable professionalism. Just as anger won't help, guilt won't do you much good, either. In fact, it has the reverse effect and keeps you trapped. As we said in the Pleaser chapter, guilt is the gift that keeps on giving. In Pleaser's case, guilt is blackmail to keep you pleasing others. For Con Artist it produces the self-defeating behaviors you're stuck in and justifies the excessive drinking needed to kill off the guilt feelings. Your gift is a neatly wrapped excuse to down another twelve-pack. Read the following stress tips to learn how to deal with difficult life changes.

Compartmentalize, don't deny.

Deal with issues one at a time by compartmentalizing. Focus on one and put the others out of sight for a while. Select the most pressing. Then visualize placing the other problems in a computer file and pressing "Save." When you've grappled with and begin to feel some mastery of one, open the file and take out another to work on. This is not to be confused with Con Artist denial, in which you simply bury concerns under a pile of beer cans and never go back and dig them out. Compartmentalizing reduces stress because it keeps you from feeling overwhelmed and encourages handling difficulties in increments.

Maintain old relationships and reach out for new ones.

Deal with your loneliness. Stay in touch with your children and old friends. You need the anchor of contact with your loved ones. Establish new relationships. Barhopping with Inner Con Artist seldom brings lasting connections. Consider group therapy. The kinds of relationships people develop in group are based on mutual support of others who are also trying to change. Seek out friends with whom you can share hobbies and interests. Most large companies also have activities groups. There is a tendency to withdraw when going through as much change as losing your family and moving to a new state. You're like an injured wolf who holes up in his den to lick his wounds. Reach out, and instead of prowling the bars, hunt for positive, nourishing relationships and activities.

Build on your existing competencies to attain job satisfaction.

Increase your job skills and competency through training on your job. It's likely your company has training to teach you new skills you're expected to learn. Presentation methods and customer relations are popular corporate training programs and would be valuable for you. Instead of recoiling in horror at multitasking, seek out those who are good at it and learn from them. Training will increase your sense of competency, which will decrease your need to rely on Inner Con Artist. A new perception is that your job is a challenge that you can use to help get yourself unstuck. Expanding your knowledge base will pull you out of the mire.

Stress Tips Summary

All the stress tips in this reply show Twelve-Pack how to face his difficulties rather than sidestep them. He can work toward positive change when he stops anesthetizing his painful emotions. He'll begin to deal with his flawed personal relationships and improve his work skills with on-the-job training.

TOPIC SUMMARY

Coping With the Stress of Change

Dear Readers,

We've talked about how other Stress Personalities cope with the stress of painful experiences such as massive, sudden life changes. Worrier for example, envisions the worst possible outcome. Con Artist helps insure the worst possible outcome by numbing you to painful emotions related to change.

When you don't deal with personal setbacks, especially the kinds of jolting shocks Twelve-Pack went through, it's bound to affect work performance. It's interesting to note in his letter that though he lost his family, job, and friend, he identified the new job as his real difficulty. His woes will continue until he acknowledges and grapples with the strong emotions barely under the surface that are spiking his stressometer.

Most people don't like to face difficult personal problems, but it's necessary. Six out of ten people who march down the aisle later march into divorce court. A divorce is traumatic and can get ugly. Tempers flare, and behavior people would never ordinarily exhibit spews out. No wonder Inner Con Artist doesn't want to have anything to do with all these complex and agonizing distractions. Besides, this part of you is not capable of handling them.

This Stress Personality hides things not only from others but from yourself. Troubles are minimized with statements like, "Oh, it's not that big a deal," and "You're making more out of it than you need to." These denial messages make it hard for you to take yourself seriously enough to ask for help and address thorny issues.

Dealing with life's wrenching difficulties produces growth. Though it may be painful, it takes strength and builds character to figure out a way through a problem and out the other side. Even though this Stress Personality tries to help the best way it knows how, it interferes with growth. As you learn how to solve tough personal issues, you acquire skills, just as training helps improve skills at work. Since Con Artist is no good at this stuff anyway, encourage this part of yourself to go play while you, the grown-up, take over.

~~~~~~~~~~~~~~~~~~~~~~~~~~~~~~~~~~~~

POSTSCRIPT

Outwitting The Trickster

Dear Readers,

People don't like to admit to the Inner Con Artist in themselves, but our society encourages the behavior. States pass draconian drunk-driving laws but allow gas stations to sell beer and wine. The popularity of lotteries is a prime example of state-promoted Inner Con Artist activity. Gambling can be an addiction every bit as expensive and destructive as drug dependency. And the odds of winning the lottery are infinitesimal, yet millions play all the time under the illusory and hopeful dream they'll strike it rich. "After I win the lottery" has become a national aphorism for people expressing their Inner Con Artist dream of getting something for nothing.

It's easy to excuse your own Inner Con Artist, because you see the behavior all around you. It has the cachet of cultural approval, yet people are also punished for it. So there is always an inner conflict, especially when you take this Stress Personality to work.

The Inner Con Artist Quandary

You battle with this Stress Personality because it isn't trustworthy and can't be counted on to keep its promises and contracts. You can get into the same struggle with the company you work for if you think they are not acting honorably. Every day you read about hundreds of thousands laid off in downsizings despite record corporate profits. Companies "restructure" by firing workers then hire them back at lower wages and reduced benefits. Employee pension funds are plundered by corporate raiders. Workers nearing retirement are terminated to avoid paying pensions. Viewed through the eyes of Inner Con Artist, the question becomes, "Why should I be accountable when the organization I work for can't be counted on?"

At this point you have a choice of options. As we've seen in this chapter, those who chose the Inner Con Artist response paid for it with severe stress. You have to choose how you want to respond to this fact of contemporary work life. It's a question of values. Do you choose your behavior in response to someone else's? Or do you choose to be the way you are because that's who you want to be?

You can rebel at work through Con Artist by doing just enough to get by or through other rebellious acts. Those who are clever at pulling it off are often successful in that they keep their jobs. By contrast, many hard-working, driven people who give their all to companies are fired through no fault of their own.

If hard work equaled guaranteed employment, there would be no quandary. But as the song goes, "It ain't necessarily so." One veteran manager, in reply to the question, "What's the best guarantee of promotion in this company?" said, "Get to know somebody in a high position who can further your career, adapt his or her values, and regurgitate them as your own." Loyalty, hard work, competency, and good deeds weren't mentioned. If that manager is right, superficiality and deception, both of which Con Artist excels at, are necessary for corporate success. You're now right back in the quandary again. If hard work isn't rewarded, why bother? It's back to your value system. How you approach your job is up to you, but remember, you always have to live with yourself. But which self are you choosing to live with? Inner Con Artist is just as adept at fooling you as it is others.

The Dream Trickster

Inner Con Artist is the wily trickster of mythology. This trickster is not a "bad guy" but usually gets a bad rap. The struggle with Con Artist often surfaces in dreams. The theme, around which many variations are built, involves a grinning, seedy-looking character who has invaded your space and won't leave.

For example, the scene could be your home. You walk into the living room to find this interloper sitting in your favorite chair drinking beer and plunking the empty bottles down on your prized coffee table, causing ugly moisture rings. You feel outraged and incensed and you angrily order this invader to leave immediately. He not only ignores you, but laughs at you for thinking you could have any influence over him. You might even get so angry that you start punching the bum, but it has no effect.

He keeps laughing and swilling beer. You wake up shaking with anger, indignation, and a sense of futility. This dream reflects the unconscious power of Inner Con Artist and the disgust and helplessness you feel at trying to control this part of yourself. When you start dealing openly with Inner Con Artist, these dreams go away. So the dreams are an excellent tip-off that you're not dealing with the behavior pattern. You can't bargain with this elusive Stress Personality, because it will agree to anything you want and do what it wants anyway. Inner Con Artist has no conscience, so you can't shame it into behaving. It's not rational, so it's impossible to reason it out of its caprices. You can't beat it up, because it only laughs at you. Con Artist will always point you down easy street, even if you have to be carried on a stretcher.

How to Avoid the Battle of Wills With *Inner Con Artist*

One of the ways you stay in this battle is by feeling guilty when you don't live up to your self-promises. The determination to change is the first declaration of war: "I am going to lose these ten pounds." Then comes the first skirmish and you lose. For example, you decide to go on a diet. You do well for the first three days. Then there's a going away party for a colleague and you eat everything in sight, although you announced beforehand, "I won't be eating much because I'm on a diet."

Right now is the point at which you have a choice to disengage from the battle with Con Artist or not. You say, "Oh, I'm so weak. Look at me; I can never stick to anything; there's no hope for me." Next you plunge into vats of oozing guilt. This proves that you're so hopelessly weak, what's the point of even trying to change?

Instead, don't take the bait of guilt, because it's the penance you pay for continuing the Inner Con Artist behavior. If you feel guilty, you've paid the price for being "bad" and can continue to drift down easy street. Refuse to feel this way. If you fall off the diet wagon, get right back on. For those of you who recognize this battle, you'll be surprised how hard it is to eliminate the guilt. But now that you know what links you to the tug-of-war with Con Artist, you have to be relentless in repudiating regret. If you find you can't at first, then at least acknowledge that you're choosing to continue the battle.

Another way to trick the trickster when tempted to indulge in a no-no is to agree with Con Artist that the temptation is indeed alluring. Instead of saying no, you say yes but with the stipulation that you can have it, but not just now. Then you envision tubs of ice cream, great sheets of choco-late, and a Big Rock Candy Mountain and say to your Con Artist, "Don't worry; there's lots of it, and we can always have some later." This method speaks directly to the deprivation Con Artist feels and addresses the fear that you won't get your share. It also tempers the impulsivity of this Stress Personality, and after the initial surge of desire, it recedes.

In our workshops we find that very few people openly identify or take on their Inner Con Artist at first. In contrast, follow-up work with the same people often centers on this Stress Personality and how to handle it. Once they begin using the Stress Personalities Model, they notice the pat-tern for the first time, have a name for it, and realize it's a normal though troublesome part of themselves. Then they are ready to confront this elu-sive "now you see it, now you don't" trickster.

QUICK-REFERENCE STRESS TIPS FOR *INNER CON ARTIST*

Use these stress tips to manipulate Inner Con Artist out of self-defeating behavior:

- Shape up.
- Deal with things as they arise rather than ignore them.
- To defeat procrastination, tackle one task a day.
- To regain self-respect, keep promises made to self and others.
- Take responsibility.
- Challenge Con Artist self-defeating rationalizations.
- When you get off track, reject guilt and get back on.
- Avoid a battle of wills with Inner Con Artist.
- Be accountable to yourself.
- Overcome denial by facing issues.
- Work toward good health habits.

Epilogue

Dear Readers,

If there is one message we've attempted to get across in this book, it is that you've got to take care of yourself in today's high-stress workplace. When you give so much of your time, energy, sweat, and toil for an employer, always keep in mind that *you* are responsible for your own best interests. Work can be seductive and even an obsession. You can wear company T-shirts and drink your morning coffee from a company mug. You can succumb to the corporate culture that promotes total absorption in the job, be doggedly loyal and devoted, work killer schedules, and merge your identity with that of your company. But take heed: According to economist Milton Friedman, the corporation's only responsibility is to make a profit. We add to that, "and not to see that employees live a healthy, well-balanced life."

So it's in your best interest to recognize how your Stress Personalities contribute to job stress. They are, after all, parts of *you*. It's best if they are not strangers but familiar energies you can balance, harness, or direct. Take the stress tests again when you feel overwhelmed. They will indicate which Stress Personalities have emerged. Then go over the stress tips and quick-reference guides. Choose one tip that applies in your case or one from the appropriate reference guide and put it into practice right away. Then add others that may apply.

It's only natural in reading this book that you will concentrate on the Stress Personalities you most immediately recognize in yourself. But because Stress Personalities are normal behaviors that you tend to use in different kinds of situations, you may respond from a Stress Personality you haven't acknowledged in yourself. During the Gulf War, one young man who was in the Army Reserve was nearly paralyzed by his Worrier. It was not a Stress Personality he would have identified with just a few months earlier. He was in graduate school, working long hours, and described himself as a "full-on Striver." It wasn't until he took the Worrier assessment test that he recognized that this Stress Personality was responsible for his current stress.

Stressful situations change or differ according to circumstances. Re-taking the stress tests can help you identify which Stress Personality has emerged. It may surprise you.

We mentioned in Chapter One that it's not just a single behavior or perception that causes stress but the frequency of the stress behavior you must pay attention to. Also, the frequency with which you apply new behaviors will determine how well you manage your Stress Personalities.

For example, if Pleaser prevents you from saying no when swamped, you may choose to follow the Pleaser quick-reference stress tip, "Find a way to say no and mean it." You may not be able to start practicing this new behavior on your boss. But you'll find that if you increasingly practice saying no to those co-workers who try to take advantage of you, it will eventually become a comfortable response. When you discover that nothing terrible happens, it will be easier to say no even to those in authority.

Some of you will recognize a particularly troublesome behavior you want to change and will start by decreasing the frequency of the stress behavior and increasing that of a new behavior. Some people just stop high-stress behavior cold turkey when they recognize what they're doing. The point is to always acknowledge the changes you're making that reduce your stress. Use this book on an ongoing basis as a tool to modify stress behavior that prevents you from being the healthy, effective person you can be. You may be overworked, but you don't have to be overwhelmed or overwrought.

About the Authors

M ary Dempcy and Rene Tihista are a husband-wife team who have conducted stress and conflict resolution workshops for corporations, healthcare centers, and public agencies throughout the United States and Canada since 1977. They publish an Internet e-mail newsletter on job stress available at jobstress@aol.com. They are the authors of *Stress Personalities: A Look Inside Our Selves,* their first book on the Stress Personalities Model; *A Guide to Your Stress Personalities* stress workbook; *Conflict Management Skills For Managers* workbook; and two cassette tapes. All are available through Stress Personalities Publications, P.O. Box 1538, Sisters, OR 97759; (541) 383-4130, phone/fax; e-mail 03255@worldlink.com.